BORN AGAIN
TO A LIVING HOPE

A MESSIANIC COMMENTARY ON 1 PETER

Born Again to a Living Hope: A Messianic Commentary on 1 Peter
The Messianic Jewish Application Commentary Series

Author: David Wilber
Series Editor: Dr. Igal German

Copyright © 2025 David Wilber.
Published by Pronomian Publishing.

All rights reserved. No part of this book may be reproduced, stored in a retrieval system, or transmitted in any form or by any means—electronic, mechanical, photocopying, recording, or otherwise—without prior written permission of the publisher, except in the case of brief quotations embodied in critical articles and reviews. Request for permission to reproduce more than 300 words can be made at **www.pronomianpublishing.com/**

Pronomian Publishing LLC
Clover, SC 29710

Published in the United States of America.

Scripture quotations are from the ESV® Bible (The Holy Bible, English Standard Version®), © 2001 by Crossway, a publishing ministry of Good News Publishers. ESV Text Edition: 2025. The ESV text may not be quoted in any publication made available to the public by a Creative Commons license. The ESV may not be translated in whole or in part into any other language. Used by permission. All rights reserved. The Holy Bible, English Standard Version®, is adapted from the Revised Standard Version of the Bible, copyright Division of Christian Education of the National Council of the Churches of Christ in the U.S.A.

David Wilber's commentary on 1 Peter is a rare and valuable achievement. As a scholar who teaches and preaches both the Old and New Testaments, I can attest that 1 Peter is a crucial, and often misunderstood, bridge between them. To read Peter well, one must read the Tanakh well. Wilber navigates this territory with impressive skill and theological clarity. He masterfully avoids the common pitfall of supersessionism, demonstrating that Peter's message is not one of Israel's replacement but of the nations' inclusion into Israel's story and covenants. Wilber's Pronomian (Torah-positive) framework is a particular strength. His exegesis of the "holiness" command (1 Pet. 1:16) is rightly grounded in its original Levitical context, and his handling of the "royal priesthood" (1 Pet. 2:9) correctly connects it to God's promises of restoration. This is a commentary that takes the Hebrew Scriptures as seriously as Peter did. Combining solid academic arguments, like his robust defense of Petrine authorship, with warm, practical application, Wilber has created a resource that is at once deep and accessible. *Born Again to a Living Hope* is a vital contribution for pastors, students, and laypeople, and it will be a welcome guide for any believer seeking to understand this foundational epistle.
—Matthew C. Nappier, Ph.D.

Few commentaries succeed in combining rigorous research with cutting-edge scholarship while also encouraging the reader's faith. David Wilber's commentary on 1 Peter achieves this balance, prompting us to consider the text carefully in its original context and reflect on its meaning for our time.
—Ryan C. Lambert, director of the Bridge Builders Forum and author of *The Weird Apostle*

David Wilber provides interesting insight into the epistle of 1 Peter. He cites a great amount of scholarship to support his positions and offers valuable insight into the mind of Peter.
—Michael Jones, director of Inspiring Philosophy

In *Born Again to a Living Hope*, Wilber has masterfully gifted the believing community with a study on 1 Peter that perfectly balances exegetical diligence with clarity for all audiences to benefit immensely from. This short yet deeply stimulating and insightful commentary provides the reader with all they could ask for and belongs on every believer's shelf, taking its worthy place among great studies on Petrine literature.
—R. M. Bailey, author of *Whom God Has Made Clean* and *Purity, Politics, and Parables*

Contents

Acknowledgements vii
Abbreviations ix

MJAC Series Introduction 1
Author's Preface 5
Introduction to 1 Peter 7

1. To Those God Has chosen (1 Peter 1:1–2) 19
2. An Everlasting Inheritance (1 Peter 1:3–12) 27
3. Be Holy (1 Peter 1:13–25) 35
4. You Are God's People (1 Peter 2:1–10) 45
5. Live Honorably Among the Gentiles (1 Peter 2:11–3:7) 59
6. Suffer for Righteousness' Sake (1 Peter 3:8–22) 73
7. The End of All Things is At Hand (1 Peter 4:1–11) 89
8. Persevere through Suffering (1 Peter 4:12–19) 101
9. Clothe Yourselves with Humility (1 Peter 5:1–5) 109
10. After You Have Suffered a Little While (1 Peter 5:6–14) ... 117

About the Author 125
About the Editor 127
Bibliography 129

Acknowledgments

I am deeply grateful to my wife and children, whose love encourages me to keep studying and working hard. I also thank my colleagues (and dear friends), Dr. Igal German and Mark Jacob, for their helpful insights and scholarship. Above all, I offer thanks and praise to Yeshua the Messiah, through whom I have been born again to a living hope. To him belongs all the glory.

Abbreviations

ABCS	Ariel's Bible Commentary	NIBCNT	New International Bible Commentary on the New Testament
AUSS	Andrews University Seminary Studies		
BDAG	Danker, Frederick W., Walter Bauer, William F. Arndt, and F. Wilbur Gingrich. Greek-English Lexicon of the New Testament and Other Early Christian Literature. 4th ed. Chicago: University of Chicago Press, 2021.	NIVAC	NIV Application Commentary
		NCBC	New Cambridge Bible Commentary
		NTS	New Testament Studies
		PCNT	Paideia Commentaries on the New Testament
		TBC	Torch Bible Commentaries
		TNTC	Tyndale New Testament Commentaries
BECNT	Baker Exegetical Commentary on the New Testament	TWOT	Harris, R. Laird., Gleason L. Archer, Jr., Bruce K. Waltke. Theological Wordbook of the Old Testament. Chicago: Moody Press, 1980.
BJPS	British Journal of Political Science		
BJS	The British Journal of Sociology		
JAE	Journal of African Economies		
JDE	Journal of Development Economics	VCSup	Supplements to Vigiliae Christianae
JEEA	Journal of the European Economic Association	WBC	Word Biblical Commentary
		WLQ	Wisconsin Lutheran Quarterly
JSNT	Journal for the Study of the New Testament	WUNT	Wissenschaftliche Untersuchungen zum Neuen Testament
JTS	The Journal of Theological Studies	ZECOT	Zondervan Exegetical Commentary on the Old Testament
NAC	The New American Commentary		

MJAC Series Introduction

With so many commentary series already in print, why introduce another one? The reason is simple: we recognized the need for a series authored by Messianic Jewish and Gentile scholars that uniquely combines detailed and rigorous biblical exegesis with practical insights for modern-day application. This distinctive blend equips readers with a deep understanding of the text's original meaning and its application in our lives today, empowering them to live out their faith in a practical and meaningful way.

At the core of our approach is a unique Messianic perspective that is dedicated to restoring the Jewish context of Scripture. By situating the text within its original cultural and historical context, this perspective not only enhances our understanding of the text but also strengthens our connection to the roots of our faith. It highlights the beautiful continuity between the Hebrew Scriptures and the New Testament, inviting both Jewish and Gentile believers to delve into God's Word and apply it faithfully in their lives today.

Terminology

Readers will encounter some unique Messianic terminology that carries significant historical weight. For example, our authors refer to the Messiah Jesus by his Hebrew name, Yeshua. Other terms we use include Torah (the Law of Moses), Tanakh (the Hebrew Bible, often called the "Old Testament"), and Shabbat (the Sabbath), among others. The use of this terminology is not merely a stylistic preference but an effort to recapture, in part, the religious and cultural context of the earliest Jewish believers in the first century. By using the same terms as the apostles and Yeshua's earliest followers, who were Jewish followers of Israel's Messiah, we can connect to a rich historical tradition and better understand their beliefs and practices.

Authorship and Perspective

The contributors to this series include both Jewish and Gentile followers of Yeshua. The original Messianic movement, with its diverse and welcoming community, has continued to this day. While the first followers of Yeshua were Jews, Gentiles were not only welcomed but also embraced a way of life centered on Israel's Messiah and the Hebrew Scriptures. In that same spirit, the voices here reflect this continuity. Whatever their personal background, each author writes from a Messianic perspective, carrying the first-century Messianic movement forward into the present day.

A Pronomian Perspective

This series is unapologetically pronomian, meaning it upholds the authority and relevance of the Torah canonically, theologically, and practically. Unlike antinomianism, which rejects the Torah's place in the life of believers today, we hold that the Law of Moses, along with the rest of Scripture, remains in effect. Within Messianic Judaism, there are nuanced discussions about how the Torah is to be lived out today. These discussions are not static, but dynamic and ongoing, engaging entire Messianic Jewish and Christian communities. They are not just historical debates, but a living tradition that you, as a reader, are part of. For example, should specific commandments apply to Gentile believers in the same way they do to Jews? Understandably, there is a range of perspectives on this matter, including among our own contributors. Nevertheless, while interpretations may vary in detail, this series as a whole takes a pronomian approach to Scripture,

MJAC Series Introduction

emphasizing the importance of the Torah in New Testament theology and inviting you to be part of this living tradition.

Pronomian hermeneutics, as employed in The Messianic Jewish Application Commentary, reflects the significant paradigm shift currently unfolding in biblical studies. This shift moves away from antinomian paradigms of theological subjectivity toward a hermeneutic that affirms the Torah's validity and relevance for Jews, Christians, and Messianic Jews. Historically, antinomian readings of the New Testament have dominated Christian theology for centuries, often with anti-Jewish overtones. However, the emergence of Messianic Jewish scholarship over the past four decades has necessitated a reassessment of the Torah's perceived obsolescence or abrogation in New Testament theology. In keeping with those exciting developments in biblical scholarship, The Messianic Jewish Application Commentary brings forth intriguing new perspectives.

A Post-Supersessionist Perspective

The Messianic Jewish Application Commentary Series also approaches the Scriptures from a post-supersessionist perspective. Supersessionism—the erroneous belief that the Church has replaced Israel—has historically led to both misinterpretations of Scripture and tragic consequences for the Jewish people. By contrast, a post-supersessionist stance not only challenges this belief but also affirms the continuing, significant role of Israel in God's purposes. We are convinced that a post-supersessionist approach is not just faithful to Scripture, but also plays a vital role in shaping the understanding and practice of the broader Body of Messiah.

In alignment with the latest developments in post-supersessionist scholarship, as seen in new theological initiatives like The New Testament after Supersessionism, The Society for Post-Supersessionist Theology, and Faith Defenders International, The Messianic Jewish Application Commentary offers fresh and intellectually stimulating readings of supposedly

MJAC Series Introduction

supersessionist New Testament passages. This approach, which engages with the Hebrew Bible, Second Temple Judaism, and Jewish Studies, underscores the scholarly context and academic rigor of the post-supersessionist perspective.

Structure

Each chapter in the series follows a consistent format. It starts with an exegesis section, a verse-by-verse exposition that uncovers the original meaning of the text. This is followed by an application section, a practical reflection on how the text can be lived out in our lives today. This structure, with its explicit goal of deepening faith and discipleship, ensures that each commentary connects the world of the Bible with the practical realities of modern discipleship.

It is our prayer that the insights shared here deepen your personal relationship with God, strengthen your walk with Yeshua, and enrich your participation in the life of his people. As you journey through these volumes, may you be continually reminded of the faithfulness of the God of Israel and be blessed in every way as you seek to live out his truth.

—Dr. Igal German, Series Editor

Author's Preface

How do we remain faithful to God in an ungodly world that opposes our beliefs and values? The apostle Peter addresses this question in his first epistle. Writing to persecuted believers scattered throughout Asia Minor, Peter urges them to remain steadfast in their faith, even though they are facing hardship and social rejection. Why? Because their everlasting inheritance is far more precious than any cultural acceptance or comfort the world can offer. Peter reminds them that the living hope secured through the Messiah's resurrection gives them reason to rejoice, even while they are suffering.

I believe the Spirit-inspired instruction found in Peter's epistle remains just as relevant today as it was then. Like Peter's original readers, we are learning to navigate the tension between faithfully serving God and being good citizens of a society that rejects his ways. We often experience conflict with the world as we seek to uphold God's truth and moral standards revealed in Scripture. Yet, like those early believers, we can draw strength from the living hope into which we have been "born" through the Messiah's resurrection—a hope that moves us to rejoice in spite of trials. Following the Messiah's own example (1 Pet. 2:21), we can embrace suffering with the assurance that we will be vindicated along with him.

My prayer is that God will use this commentary to strengthen your faith and remind you of the inheritance "kept in heaven for you" (1 Pet. 1:4). With Peter I proclaim, "Though you do not now see him, you believe in him and rejoice with a joy that is inexpressible and filled with glory" (1 Pet. 1:8). The Messiah will indeed return to save his people. In the meantime, "set your hope fully on the grace that will be brought to you" and "be holy in all your conduct, since it is written, 'You shall be holy, for I am holy'" (1 Pet. 1:13, 15–16).

Introduction to 1 Peter

The epistle of 1 Peter delivers an important message of hope and provides instruction for believers who are facing opposition for their beliefs and values. Drawing from the Hebrew Scriptures (Old Testament) and the example of Yeshua, the author calls on God's people to pursue holiness and to rejoice in spite of their suffering. He reassures them that they have been "born again to a living hope" through the Messiah's resurrection, which has secured their everlasting inheritance and future salvation.

Before we study the content of this epistle, we will take some time to consider its authorship, date, and original recipients.

Authorship

Who wrote 1 Peter? According to the epistle itself, it was authored by "Peter, an apostle of Jesus Christ" (1 Pet. 1:1). Peter was one of Yeshua's original twelve disciples and a prominent leader within the early Messianic Jewish movement.[1] However, some scholars question whether the apostle Peter actually wrote 1 Peter and offer various objections to that idea. Before addressing their objections, I will first explain the reasons for accepting the epistle's claim that Peter himself was its author.[2]

First, 1 Peter had a significant impact on early Christian literature and was widely accepted as authored by Peter from the time it first circulated

---

1 The next chapter will take a closer look at Peter's background.
2 Although pseudepigraphical writings were common in antiquity, as Craig S. Keener observes, the majority of ancient letters were, in fact, written by the individuals they claim as authors. Thus, "by normal standards the burden of proof should remain with those who contest the authorial claim of 1 Pet. 1:1, which if taken at face value at least is more apt to support Petrine authorship than contest it" (*1 Peter: A Commentary* [Grand Rapids: Baker Academic, 2021], 9).

Introduction to 1 Peter

among the early Christian communities.³ That is to say, the early Christians believed that Peter wrote this epistle.⁴ For example, Polycarp's letter to the Philippians, dated around 135 CE, frequently quotes and alludes to 1 Peter (e.g., Phil. 1:3; 2:1; 8:1–2).⁵ Other second-century Christian writers, like Irenaeus, directly quote the epistle and affirm Peter's authorship (*Against Heresies* 4.9.2).⁶ Similarly, in the early third century, Tertullian quotes 1 Peter and attributes it to the apostle Peter (*Scorpiace* 12).⁷ By the early fourth century, church historian Eusebius records that Papias, Clement of Alexandria, and Origen all attributed the letter to Peter (*Church History* 2.15.2; 3:39:16; 6.25.8). Eusebius himself places 1 Peter among the "undisputed" writings of the New Testament (*Church History* 3.3.1; 3.4.2).⁸ Finally, the author of 2 Peter—who also identifies himself as Peter (2 Pet. 1:1)—refers to his epistle as "the second letter that I am writing to you" (2 Pet. 3:1). This mention of a second letter implies the existence of a first, which is "probably a reference to what we call 1

---

3   See J. Ramsay Michaels: "Aside from the four Gospels and the letters of Paul, the external attestation for 1 Peter is as strong, or stronger, than that of any other NT book" (*1 Peter*, WBC (Waco: Word, 1988), xxxiv).

4   See Keener, *1 Peter*, 17: "It is highly unlikely that early authors would quote from 1 Peter if they believed the letter to be spurious. One cannot suppose, as some do with early allusions to the Gospels, that those who used the work were ignorant of its authorship claim; the claim is explicit in 1 Pet. 1:1."

5   Kenneth Berding provides a list of fourteen "almost certain," "probable," and "possible" citations and allusions to 1 Peter in Polycarp's epistle. See Kenneth Berding, *Polycarp and Paul: An Analysis of Their Literary and Theological Relationship in Light of Polycarp's Use of Biblical and Extra-biblical Literature*, VCSup 62 (Boston: Brill, 2002), 201–201. See also Keener, *1 Peter*, 17–19.

6   D. A. Carson & Douglas J. Moo, *An Introduction to the New Testament* (Grand Rapids: Zondervan, 2005), 641. See also Keener, *1 Peter*, 23.

7   Thomas R. Schreiner, *1, 2 Peter, Jude*, NAC (Nashville: B&H Publishing, 2003), 22. Schreiner also points out possible parallels to 1 Peter in 1 Clement and the Didache, though he acknowledges that the evidence is not strong enough to definitively conclude that these authors were drawing from 1 Peter.

8   Carson & Moo, *An Introduction*, 641.

Peter."⁹ This serves as another early witness to the existence of a previous letter attributed to Peter that was well known and accepted as genuine at the time 2 Peter was written.¹⁰ From the earliest available evidence, it is clear that the first generations of Christians viewed 1 Peter as a genuine epistle authored by the apostle Peter. This widespread and early acceptance strongly supports the conclusion that it is authentic.¹¹

A second point worth mentioning is that the content of 1 Peter closely parallels Peter's sayings found elsewhere, particularly in the speeches attributed to him in the Book of Acts.¹² Both share key themes, including the fulfillment of prophecy (Acts 2:16ff; 1 Pet. 1:10–12), the death of the Messiah on a "tree" (Acts 5:30; 10:39; 1 Pet. 2:24), the Messiah as the "cornerstone" (Acts 4:11; 1 Pet. 2:7), and the connection between the Messiah's resurrection and his exaltation (Acts 2:32–36; 1 Pet. 1:21).¹³ These similarities are what we would expect if the same Peter who spoke in Acts also authored 1 Peter.

In sum, a range of historical sources—from 2 Peter to Christian writings from the second and third centuries—affirm Peter's authorship of 1 Peter. Additionally, the teachings attributed to Peter elsewhere in the New Testament closely align with the themes and content of this epistle. It should not be surprising, then, that "Petrine authorship was virtually undisputed until nineteenth-century criticism and was still widely defended afterward."¹⁴ Nevertheless, many modern scholars consider the epistle to be pseudonymous (i.e., attributed to Peter to bolster the epistle's authority, but actually written by a later author using Peter's name). Let us now address some of the reasons they give for this conclusion.

---

9   Carson & Moo, *An Introduction*, 641.
10 Keener, *1 Peter*, 24.
11 Keener, *1 Peter*, 9. See also Schreiner, *1, 2 Peter, Jude*, 22: "the external evidence for 1 Peter being authentic is quite early, and no doubts were raised about its authenticity."
12 This point is argued by Robert H. Gundry in *A Survey of the New Testament*, 5th ed. (Grand Rapids: Zondervan, 2012), 522.
13 Gundry, *Survey*, 525. See also Keener, *1 Peter*, 13n71.
14 Keener, *1 Peter*, 24.

Introduction to 1 Peter

One argument for viewing 1 Peter as pseudonymous is "its elegant Greek and rhetoric."[15] Peter's writing seems unusually polished for someone described as an "uneducated" (Acts 4:13) Galilean fisherman whose native language was Aramaic. However, the high-quality Greek of the letter is hardly sufficient grounds to dismiss Peter's authorship. First, it is reasonable to assume that Peter's command of Greek would have improved over time, especially through years of ministry to Greek-speaking audiences.[16] Peter is described as uneducated in his early life, but not unintelligent. More importantly, it was common practice in the ancient world to use an amanuensis (a scribal assistant), who often had a hand in shaping the wording and style of a document. Keener writes, "As a prominent leader, Peter would certainly have ready access to scribal and stylistic assistance."[17] In fact, Peter explicitly references the help of Silvanus in 1 Peter 5:12, who was a Roman citizen (Acts 16:37) and likely fluent in Greek and well educated.[18] If Peter had help from an amanuensis—whether Silvanus or someone else—then the epistle's polished Greek and rhetorical style could be attributed to that person's expertise.[19] In any case, the quality of the Greek in the epistle does not in any way preclude Peter from being its author.

A second argument for viewing 1 Peter as pseudonymous is the author's use of the Septuagint for quoting Scripture. Critics suggest that, given Peter's Jewish background, he would have been more likely to use the Hebrew Scriptures rather than a Greek translation.[20] However, according to Keener, "such an argument is quite weak." As Keener observes, "When composing in Greek, one will normally use the Greek

---

15 Duane F. Watson, "First Peter," in *First and Second Peter*, by Duane F. Watson and Terrance Callan, PCNT (Grand Rapids: Baker Academic, 2012), 4.
16 Watson, "First Peter," 4.
17 Keener, *1 Peter*, 10.
18 There is ongoing debate over whether Silvanus contributed to the composition of the letter or simply served as a courier. See Keener, *1 Peter*, 12.
19 Keener, *1 Peter*, 11.
20 Watson, "First Peter," 4.

translation available to one's audience. In both Rome and Asia Minor this would be the basic text-type that we generally call the Septuagint."[21] In other words, if Peter's audience primarily spoke Greek rather than Hebrew, it stands to reason that they would be acquainted with the Greek Scriptures, and thus Peter would naturally use those same Greek texts when writing to them.

A third argument for viewing 1 Peter as pseudonymous is that the content of 1 Peter appears to reflect a period later than Peter's lifetime.[22] Specifically, the epistle references Christian persecution, yet widespread, organized persecution of Christians is generally believed to have emerged much later.[23] However, while this objection to 1 Peter's authenticity was popular in the past, it is now "generally discounted" by scholars.[24] It is true that widespread, state-sponsored persecution of Christians did not occur until later, but Christians still faced various forms of hostility before 64 CE.[25] A closer look at the type of persecution described in 1 Peter suggests that believers were not yet experiencing official, empire-wide oppression. The letter points primarily to less intense forms of persecution such as slander and false accusations (1 Pet. 2:12, 15; 3:9, 16; 4:12, 16), rather than to the severe forms of persecution typically associated with state-driven efforts. According to Paul J. Achtemeier, the opposition Peter's audience faced was "due more to unofficial harassment than to official policy, more local than regional, and more at the imitation of the general populace as the result of reaction against the lifestyle of the Christians than at the initiation of Roman officials because of some general policy of seeking out and punishing Christians."[26] Con-

---

21 Keener, *1 Peter*, 16.
22 See Karen H. Jobes: "There is virtual unanimity that the apostle Peter died in Rome in the mid-60s during the reign of Emperor Nero" (*1 Peter*, BECNT [Grand Rapids: Baker Academic, 2005], 8n1).
23 Watson, "First Peter," 5.
24 Carson & Moo, *An Introduction*, 642.
25 Watson, "First Peter," 5.
26 Paul J. Achtemeier, *1 Peter*, Hermeneia (Minneapolis: Fortress Press, 1996), 35–36.

sequently, 1 Peter actually appears to reflect a period *before* Christians were targeted by formal Roman policy.[27] This suggests the epistle was likely written shortly before Nero's official persecution began,[28] making it entirely plausible that Peter could have been its author.

A fourth argument against Peter's authorship of 1 Peter claims that the use of "Babylon" as a coded reference to Rome (1 Pet. 5:13) suggests that the letter was written after 70 CE. Since Rome destroyed the temple in 70 CE as Babylon had centuries earlier, this connection became prominent in Jewish writings after that event. However, as Keener notes, "while it is true that Jews after 70 recognized the parallel particularly emphatically, it is mistaken to insist that few envisioned this parallel beforehand. Jewish interpreters during the time of the Roman Empire understood Daniel's fourth kingdom, the ultimate successor of Babylon, as Rome. They did not need to await the temple's destruction to view Rome as their Babylon-like oppressor."[29]

With Keener, I believe "the external evidence is sufficiently strong to make the case compelling for Petrine authorship."[30] In contrast, the objections raised against Peter's authorship are unpersuasive.[31] Based on

---

Achtemeier adds, "That does not rule out the possibility that persecutions occurred over large areas of the empire; they surely did, but they were spasmodic and broke out at different times in different places, the result of the flare-up of local hatreds rather than because Roman officials were engaged in the regular discharge of official policy."

27 Jobes, *1 Peter*, 8–10.

28 See Norman Hillyer: "Peter's exhortation to good citizenship (2:13–14) is enough to reject suggestions of official Roman policy against Christians at this date. On the contrary, it implies that Peter was writing his letter before the emperor Nero had changed from the public's darling on his accession in A.D. 54 to the monster he became following the outbreak on 19 July 64 of the great fire of Rome, which he later tried to blame on the Christians" (*1 and 2 Peter, Jude*, NIBCNT [Peabody, MA: Hendrickson, 1992], 3).

29 Keener, *1 Peter*, 27.

30 Keener, *1 Peter*, 9.

31 For more detailed discussion of additional objections and responses regarding Peter's authorship of 1 Peter, see Carson and Moo, *An Introduction*, 641–646; Watson, "First Peter," 3–5; Jobes, *1 Peter*, 6–14; Keener, *1 Peter*, 8–16; Schreiner, *1, 2 Peter, Jude*, 22–36.

this, let us proceed with confidence that 1 Peter was indeed written by the apostle himself.

Date and Provenance

The dating of the epistle is connected to the question of its authorship. Scholars who reject Peter's authorship will often date the epistle "as late as the early second century."[32] In contrast, those who believe Peter wrote the epistle (or that it was composed by an amanuensis writing under his direct supervision) generally date it to the early 60s CE, prior to when Christians became the target of official persecution under Nero.[33] Given the strong evidence in support of Peter's direct involvement in writing the epistle, a date around CE 63 or 64 seems most appropriate.

Where did Peter write from? At the end of the epistle, Peter sends greetings from "Babylon," which is widely understood by scholars to be a symbolic reference to Rome.[34] Additionally, Eusebius records a mid-second-century tradition from Clement of Alexandria, which attests that Peter wrote the epistle while in Rome (*Church History* 2.15.2).[35] Thus, 1 Peter was likely written in Rome sometime in CE 63 or early 64, just before Nero's persecution of Christians began.[36]

---

32 Carson & Moo, *An Introduction*, 646.
33 See Hillyer, *1 Peter*, 3: "Assuming traditional authorship for 1 Peter, the most likely date for its writing appears to be about A.D. 63, immediately before the troubles in Rome flared up under Nero."
34 See Jobes, *1 Peter*, 340: "There is virtually unanimous agreement among modern interpreters that the referent of 'Babylon' is actually Rome."
35 Watson, "First Peter," 6–7.
36 See C. E. B. Cranfield: "On the assumption that the traditional attribution of the Epistle to Peter is correct, the date must have been shortly before the Neronian persecution (in which most porobably the apostle lost his life), i.e. in AD 63 or early in 64, and the place of writing Rome" (*I & II Peter and Jude: Introduction and Commentary*, TBC [London: SCM Press, 1960], 17).

Introduction to 1 Peter

Recipients

Peter addressed his letter to followers of the Messiah Yeshua residing in "Pontus, Galatia, Cappadocia, Asia, and Bithynia"—all Roman provinces located in Asia Minor (modern-day Turkey).[37] He mentions that preachers announced the "good news" to his readers, and they embraced the message (1 Pet. 1:12).[38] But who exactly were these believers to whom Peter wrote? Were they Jewish, Gentile, or mixed communities made up of both Jews and Gentiles?

Scholars who believe 1 Peter's audience was predominantly Jewish often cite Paul's remark that Peter was entrusted with the gospel to the circumcised (Gal. 2:7–8). Additionally, they argue that the epistle's frequent quotations and allusions to the Hebrew Scriptures imply that the readers were well versed in Scripture and therefore likely had a Jewish background.[39] However, while Galatians 2:7–8 shows that Peter's primary mission was to Jews, this does not exclude him from ministering to Gentiles, as other passages clearly depict the Lord calling him to preach to them as well (Acts 10:34–48; 15:7). Furthermore, the audience's assumed knowledge of the Hebrew Scriptures does not require the

---

37 Carson & Moo, *An Introduction*, 647. Watson ("First Peter," 7) believes the order of these regions reflects the likely route the letter would have taken as it was circulated: "The provinces are listed in the order in which letters were delivered by the mail couriers working for the emperor and rich merchants, and likely the route Silvanus used to deliver copies of the letter. A ship sailing from Rome to this region would likely stop at Pontus, which begins the list, and the carrier could depart back to Rome from Nicomedia in Bithynia."

38 These preachers perhaps included Paul, whose ministry extended into this region. See Watson, "First Peter," 7.

39 Carson & Moo, *An Introduction*, 647. For an argument that Peter writes to a Jewish audience, see A. Boyd Luter, *The Epistle of James Within Judaism: The Earliest First-Century Window into Messianic Jewish Belief and Practice* (Eugene, OR: Wipf & Stock, 2024), 40–44. See also Arnold G. Fruchtenbaum, *The Messianic Jewish Epistles: Hebrews, James, First Peter, Second Peter, Jude*, ABCS (San Antonio, TX: Ariel Ministries, 2005), 318–321.

conclusion that they were raised in Judaism. As Keener writes, "Gentile converts may not have grown up with Scripture, but over time in the churches they would learn it."[40]

Most scholars contend that "the original recipients of 1 Peter were predominantly if not exclusively gentile in makeup."[41] Indeed, Peter urges his readers to resist the passions of their "former ignorance" (1 Pet. 1:14), a futile lifestyle inherited from their forefathers (1 Pet. 1:18). He further characterizes their past life as marked by "sensuality, passions, drunkenness, orgies, drinking parties, and lawless idolatry," and notes that they are now being maligned for refusing to "join" the Gentiles "in the same flood of debauchery" (1 Pet. 4:2–4).[42] Although the description of these believers' former way of life could conceivably apply to Jews,[43] the most natural reading suggests Gentiles with a pagan background.

In line with the majority of scholars, I will proceed with the view that the original readers of 1 Peter were mostly Gentiles who came from a pagan background. This does not mean the audience was *entirely* Gentile, but the epistle's description of their past life and present trials suggests that Peter was focused on instructing former pagans who were adjusting to their new identity as followers of the Jewish Messiah.[44] This view fits well against the historical backdrop of the imperial cult, which pervaded

---

40 Keener, *1 Peter*, 31. See also Watson, "First Peter," 7: "Their assumed familiarity with the OT can be attributed to instruction following conversion."
41 Kelly D. Liebengood, *Reading 1 Peter After Supersessionism: Jewish Apostolic Affirmation of Gentile Israelhood* (Eugene, OR: Cascade, 2025), 12. See also the works listed by Liebengood in note 5 on page 12.
42 Liebengood, *Reading 1 Peter*, 34. See also Achtemeier, *1 Peter*, 51; Carson & Moo, *An Introduction*, 647.
43 For instance, Jobes (*1 Peter*, 264) argues, "the inference that Jewish people would never participate in such unbridled practices reflects perhaps and idealized and romanticized view of Jewish devotion and piety rather than historical and sociological possibility."
44 As Liebengood (*Reading 1 Peter*, 74) puts it, "from a rhetorical standpoint…even if in actuality at the time of reading the audience was a mixed group," the intended "target audience" of the epistle was Gentile followers of Yeshua.

public life in first-century Roman society.⁴⁵ For Gentile believers, following the Messiah meant stepping away "from nearly all public forms of celebration, entertainment, leisure, and community pride"—a decision their neighbors would have viewed as "a hostile act against the gods that threatened family, neighbors, and city."⁴⁶ Within this historical context, it becomes clear why these believers faced persecution: they had stopped participating in the idolatrous and immoral practices common among their Gentile neighbors (1 Pet. 4:3–4). Their refusal to take part in these practices stirred suspicion and outrage, as it was viewed not only as disrespectful but also as a danger to social order and stability.

Although the recipients of 1 Peter are mostly Gentiles, Peter applies to them the identity, hopes, and responsibilities given to Israel in the Hebrew Scriptures. He describes them as "a chosen race, a royal priesthood, a holy nation, a people for his own possession" (1 Pet. 2:9), echoing covenant language from the Torah (Exod. 19:5–6; Deut. 7:6; 14:2). He also calls on them to "be holy" as God is holy (1 Pet. 1:15–16), repeating a command given to Israel to be distinct from the nations and consecrated to God (Lev. 11:44–45; 19:2).⁴⁷ According to Peter, these Gentile believers are brought into the community of Israel (cf. Eph 2:11–22) and share in Israel's mission and future hopes. Peter's use of these "Israel passages" for Gentile believers has led many interpreters to conclude that

---

45 See Liebengood, *Reading 1 Peter*, 63: "the cult extended to every aspect of life. Roman imperial ideology permeated civic space through the design of city structures and even city design as a whole. Public institutions such as the agora, the bouleuterion, the gymnasium, and the baths tended to be associated with the imperial cult. Imperial honorary inscriptions were placed through the city landscape. What is more, imperial ideology was expressed through entertainment—the theater, festivals, and games all promoted Roman imperial worship, and some of the events would have lasted from several days to a week or more."

46 Liebengood, *Reading 1 Peter*, 64.

47 See Liebengood, *Reading 1 Peter*, 23: "they are exhorted to live in keeping it the foundational covenant stipulations established by the God of Israel in the wilderness: 'You shall be holy, for I am holy' (1 Pet 1:15–16; Lev 11:44)."

Introduction to 1 Peter

1 Peter teaches supersessionism, which is "the traditional Christian belief that since Christ's coming the Church has taken the place of the Jewish people as God's chosen community, and that God's covenant with the Jews is now over and done."[48] It is frequently assumed that Peter is effectively reassigning Israel's identity and privileges to Gentile Christians. However, Kelly D. Liebengood explains that such a reading is mistaken:

> Peter is not taking Israel's identity, prerogatives, and mission and transferring them to the gentiles (as has often been the assumption or claim); rather, Peter is exhorting gentiles to distance themselves from their gentile culture with its assumptions, values, practices, and hopes. To be more specific, Peter is exhorting his readers to orient themselves *as gentiles* to a particularly *Jewish* way of life that is patterned after the life of Jesus (e.g., 1 Pet 2:21–23 mimicked in 1 Pet 3:9–12) and built upon the hopes and expectations of Israel…To say it another way, in 1 Peter, the gentiles who have been born-anew as a result of the resurrection of Jesus Christ (1 Pet 1:3) are ransomed from their former way of life (1 Pet 1:18) and called to learn a new culture patterned after the Messiah of Israel and shaped by the God of Israel's expectations for Israel's corporate life, but distinctly as gentiles…Read in this way, it is not that Israel has been superseded by gentile followers of Jesus. Quite the contrary…it appears that Peter is claiming that their gentile heritage (narrative self-understanding, hopes, way of life, values, etc.) has been replaced with that of "Israelhood."[49]

Indeed, Peter is not suggesting that Gentile Christians have replaced the Jewish people. The only "supersessionism" found in 1 Peter is his

---

48 R. Kendall Soulen, "Supersessionism," in *A Dictionary of Jewish-Christian Relations*, ed. Edward Kessler and Neil Wenbron (New York: Cambridge University Press, 2005), 413.
49 Liebengood, *Reading 1 Peter*, 27–28.

call for his Gentile readers to supersede their former pagan way of life with a new way of life rooted in the Messiah's example and the Hebrew Scriptures. For these Gentile believers, who were facing rejection from the broader society because of their faith in the Messiah, this message would have been especially meaningful. By identifying them as God's chosen people and giving them a place in the community of Israel, Peter offers them a new sense of purpose and belonging.

Born Again to a Living Hope

At the heart of 1 Peter is a message of hope for believers striving to remain faithful to God in a world that misunderstands and opposes them. Peter's original Gentile readers were experiencing rejection because of their faith, so he reminds them of who they truly are in God's eyes. Though rejected by society, they have been chosen by God, brought into the community of Israel, and now share in Israel's mission and hope for the future. As God's people, Peter urges them to leave behind their former way of life and embrace a life of holiness. Their living hope, secured through the Messiah's resurrection, empowers them to rejoice in the midst of suffering.

As we now turn to the text of this epistle, my prayer is that you will be encouraged to "stand firm" in your faith (1 Pet. 5:12), knowing that you, too, have been born again to a living hope.

Chapter 1

To Those God Has Chosen
(1 Peter 1:1–2)

> **1** Peter, an apostle of Jesus Christ, To those who are elect exiles of the Dispersion in Pontus, Galatia, Cappadocia, Asia, and Bithynia, **2** according to the foreknowledge of God the Father, in the sanctification of the Spirit, for obedience to Jesus Christ and for sprinkling with his blood: May grace and peace be multiplied to you.

The epistle we are studying identifies Peter as its author. But who was Peter? He was one of the twelve disciples of Yeshua the Messiah (Mark 3:16). Here, he is referred to as an apostle. The term "apostle" broadly means someone who is sent out as a representative. The Messiah himself commissioned Peter to be his representative and to carry his message.[1]

Peter's original name was Simon (*Shimon* in Hebrew). He was introduced to Yeshua by his brother Andrew, who had been a disciple of John the Baptizer (John 1:35, 40). Andrew came to believe in Yeshua after hearing John the Baptizer declare that Yeshua was the Lamb of God (John 1:36–37). When Simon was first brought to Yeshua, Yeshua gave him the Aramaic nickname *Cephas* ("rock"), which is rendered into Greek

---

[1] Craig S. Keener translates ἀπόστολος here as "commissioned agent." He writes, "Noting that the cognate verb apostellō ("send") often translates the Hebrew šālaḥ in the Greek Scriptures, many scholars cite as a (limited) analogy the Jewish conception of the commissioned agent (a šalîaḥ) who accurately represents the sender. Sometimes Jewish sources treat as agents Moses, Aaron, or biblical prophets, since they spoke on God's authority rather than their own. Peter is not great in himself, but is the agent of Christ, who is great" (*1 Peter: A Commentary* [Grand Rapids: Baker Academic, 2021], 43).

as *Petros* and into English as Peter (John 1:42).[2] Later, while Peter and Andrew were fishing, Yeshua approached them and said, "Follow me, and I will make you fishers of men" (Matt. 4:19).[3] Without hesitation, they left their nets and, from that moment on, became disciples of Yeshua.

Peter heard Yeshua's teachings firsthand and directly witnessed many of his miracles, such as the raising of Jairus's daughter and the transfiguration (Mark 5:37; Matt. 17:1–2). He boldly confessed Yeshua as the Messiah (Matt. 16:16), but also timidly denied him three times during the night of Yeshua's trial before his crucifixion (Luke 22:61–62). Yet, despite Peter's failures, the risen Messiah appeared personally to him (Luke 24:34) and called him to feed his sheep (John 21:15–17).

After Yeshua's ascension, Peter was commissioned to proclaim the glorious truth of the risen Messiah to all nations and to teach them all that Yeshua commanded (Matt 28:18–20; Acts 1:8). However, fulfilling this mission required him to confront and overcome certain unrighteous prejudices he held toward Gentiles. To address this, the Lord gave Peter a vision, teaching him not to regard anyone as unclean or common (Acts 10:9–29).[4] From then on, Peter preached to Gentiles, starting with the

---

2 Keener, *1 Peter*, 42.
3 See Craig Evans: "The point of the comparison is that in following Jesus these Galilean fishermen will no longer be pursuing fish; they will be pursuing human beings" (Craig A. Evans, *Matthew*, NCBC [New York: Cambridge University Press, 2012], 93).
4 Although Peter's vision in Acts 10 is often cited as evidence that God abolished the food laws in the Torah, a growing body of scholarship challenges that view. See, e.g., R. M. Bailey, *Whom God Has Made Clean: A Pronomian Pocket Guide to Acts 10:9–15* (Clover, SC: Pronomian Publishing, 2025); Paul T. Sloan, *Jesus and the Law of Moses: The Gospels and the Restoration of Israel within First-Century Judaism* (Grand Rapids: Baker Academic, 2025), 216–221; Colin House, "Defilement by Association: Some Insights from the Usage of κοινός/κοινόω in Acts 10 and 11," *AUSS* 21 (1983), 143–153; Clinton Wahlen, "Peter's Vision and Conflicting Definitions of Purity," *NTS* 51, no. 4 (2005): 505–518; Isaac W. Oliver, *Torah Praxis after 70 CE: Reading Matthew and Luke-Acts as Jewish Texts*, WUNT II 355 (Tübingen: Mohr Siebeck, 2013), chap. 10; Jason A. Staples, "'Rise, Kill, and Eat': Animals as Nations in Early Jewish Visionary Literature and Acts 10," *JSNT* 42.1 (2019), 10–12; Benjamin Frostad, "He Made No Distinction: Gentiles and the Role

household of Cornelius (Acts 10:34–48). Some Jewish believers criticized Peter for associating with Gentiles (Acts 11:3), but Peter explained everything that had taken place and responded, "If then God gave the same gift to them as he gave to us when we believed in the Lord Jesus Christ, who was I that I could stand in God's way?" (Acts 11:17). Peter's testimony quieted his critics' objections, and they acknowledged that God had indeed welcomed the Gentiles into the community of faith (Acts 11:18). In this way, God used Peter to open the door for the Gospel to be brought to the Gentile world.

Peter walked closely with Yeshua himself and was a key leader in the original Messianic Jewish movement that transformed the world. His instructions carry the wisdom of someone who personally experienced the cost of following the Messiah. As a Jew who faced persecution from his own people for following Yeshua, Peter understood what it meant to suffer for his faith, and he knew how to stand firm for the Gospel in the midst of overwhelming cultural pressure. He was uniquely equipped to encourage and instruct the early believers facing those same challenges, and the wisdom in his epistle continues to encourage and instruct us as we face similar trials today.

Peter addressed his epistle to "those God has chosen—resident aliens dispersed throughout the provinces of Pontus, Galatia, Cappadocia, Asia, and Bithynia" (1 Pet. 1:1).[5] Jewish people living outside the land of Israel were frequently referred to as the "dispersed" and "recognized

---

of Torah in Acts 15" (MA Thesis, Briercrest Seminary, 2021), 70–73.

5 This is Craig Keener's translation (*1 Peter*, xxxvii). The ESV quoted above has "exiles," but a more accurate translation is "resident aliens" or "visiting foreigners/strangers" (see NASB, BLB, HCSB, ERV, NET). While there are specific Greek terms for "exile" or "exiles" (αἰχμαλ-words), the terms παρεπίδημος and πάροικος (used in 1 Pet 1:1 and 2:11) are not among them. BDAG (689, 692) defines these terms as resident foreigner, stranger, or alien. Although some English translations, like the ESV, render these terms as "exiles," there is little linguistic basis for that translation. I'm grateful to New Testament scholar Logan A. Williams for sharing his insights on this topic and for generously taking the time to answer my questions via email.

themselves as God's chosen people, but often lived as resident aliens in the predominantly gentile cities where they settled."[6] However, it seems that Peter is using the terms "dispersion" and "resident aliens" as metaphors to emphasize that his readers are to view themselves as temporary residents in the world and that their permanent home is in the Messiah's eternal kingdom (1 Pet. 5:10; cf. 2 Pet. 1:11). As Craig Keener writes, "They are God's people residing as aliens in a culture foreign to their divine origin."[7]

Peter further describes his readers as those chosen "according to the foreknowledge of God the Father, in the sanctification of the Spirit, for obedience to Jesus Christ and for sprinkling with his blood" (1 Pet. 1:2). This description offers insight into Peter's understanding of the identity and calling of believers: they are chosen by God the Father, sanctified by the Spirit, and ransomed by the blood of Yeshua.[8] Just as the Messiah was "foreknown before the foundation of the world" (1 Pet. 1:20) to carry out God's plan of redemption through his death and resurrection, Peter affirms that his readers, too, are chosen according to God's purpose. As Paul A. Himes writes, "the epistles' audience and their ultimate destiny (bound up with Christ) have forever existed in the mind of God and are part of his grand master plan."[9] No matter how difficult their circumstances may appear, they are not in their situation by accident. God has a purpose for them right where they are.

Peter further explains that his readers were chosen "in the sanctification of the Spirit" (1 Pet. 1:2). As Wayne Grudem observes, "Peter is saying that his readers' whole existence as 'chosen sojourners of the

---

6   Keener, *1 Peter*, 45.
7   Keener, *1 Peter*, 45.
8   Keener (*1 Peter*, 59) suggests that the mention of Father, Spirit, and Yeshua so close together here "may presuppose a trinitarian or triadic, prototrinitarian understanding."
9   Paul A. Himes, *A Foreknown Destiny for the Socially Destitute: An Examination of 1 Peter's Concept of Foreknowledge in the Establishment of Social-Spiritual Identity* (PhD diss., Southeastern Baptist Theological Seminary, 2013), xvi.

To Those God Has Chosen (1 Peter 1:1–2)

Dispersion…' is being lived 'in' the realm of the sanctifying work of the Spirit."[10] Sanctification refers not only to the initial act of being set apart from sin and adopted into God's family through faith in the Messiah but also to the ongoing process of being conformed to his image. The Holy Spirit works within believers, causing them to become more like the holy Messiah each day. Peter reassures his readers that the "unseen, unheard activity of God's Holy Spirit surrounds them almost like a spiritual atmosphere 'in' which they live and breathe, turning every circumstance, every sorrow, every hardship into a tool for his patient sanctifying work."[11]

The plan of God and the sanctifying work of the Spirit is "for obedience to Jesus Christ and for sprinkling with his blood" (1 Pet. 1:2). That is, according to Peter, believers are chosen and sanctified so that they may walk in obedience. The phrase "for sprinkling with his blood" echoes Exodus 24:3–8, where Moses ratifies the covenant by sprinkling sacrificial blood on the people of Israel as they declare, "we will be obedient." Peter applies this same imagery to Yeshua's followers. Yeshua's blood is sprinkled upon believers (cf. Isa. 52:15), marking them as members of the covenant and calling them to be obedient to God just as Israel was at Sinai.[12]

Peter concludes his greeting with the words, "May grace and peace be multiplied to you," a common expression among believers at the time (cf. 2 Pet. 1:2; Rom. 1:7; 1 Cor. 1:3; Rev. 1:4). Peter prays that his readers experience an overflow of God's kindness and peace, even in the midst of their present hardships.

Lessons for Today: Resident Aliens in the Modern World

Like Peter's original readers, we as followers of Yeshua live as resident aliens

---

10 Wayne Grudem, *1 Peter*, TNTC (Grand Rapids: Eerdmans, 1988), 51–52.
11 Grudem, *1 Peter*, 52.
12 Keener, *1 Peter*, 60.

in the world, looking forward to the day when the Messiah returns to bring us to our true home. As the old song goes, "This world is not my home; I'm just a-passing through."[13] As we pass through this world, we find ourselves surrounded by a culture that often opposes our values and convictions. Secular society in the West frequently mocks, disparages, and excludes us because of our identity as "Christians" (1 Pet. 4:16).

To give a specific example from our modern context, we might consider how secular society often seeks to silence and penalize those who dare to hold views that go against popular public opinion. And indeed, as followers of Yeshua who stand on the truth of Scripture, we hold many views that the culture finds offensive. For instance, in today's secular society, biblical convictions about life, gender, and marriage are often met with hostility. If you affirm biblical values in these areas, you may be labeled a bigot. You might lose friendships or even face legal consequences.[14] Living as a faithful disciple in today's culture is not trendy and often can lead to conflict with the world, at times even violent conflict.

Certainly, modern Christians in the West do not face the same level of hardship as Peter's original readers. We are not subjected to overt, state-sanctioned violence as believers were in the years shortly following the writing of 1 Peter. Still, we do encounter social exclusion and disdain for the convictions we hold. Like the believers Peter addressed in his epistle, we feel out of place in a world that does not share our values, and

---

13 Jim Reeves, "This World Is Not My Home," recorded January 28, 1962, track 1 on *We Thank Thee*, RCA Victor LSP-2610, 1962, vinyl LP.

14 Take, for instance, these elderly pro-life activists who were imprisoned for their pro-life activism: Joe Bukuras, "Locked Up: Meet the Elderly and Infirm Women Now in Prison for Pro-Life Activism," *Catholic News Agency*, June 6, 2024, https://www.catholicnewsagency.com/news/257916/locked-up-meet-the-elderly-and-infirm-women-now-in-prison-for-pro-life-activism. See also the case of a man who was targeted, charged, and arrested at his home by the FBI—an action widely viewed as an attempt to intimidate pro-life activists (he was later acquitted of all charges): Brittany Bernstein, "Pro-Life Activist Arrested by FBI Acquitted on Federal Charges," *Yahoo News*, January 30, 2023, https://www.yahoo.com/news/pro-life-activist-arrested-fbi-201612330.html.

we yearn for the day when the Messiah returns to bring us home where we belong. In the meantime, we are called to engage with the world thoughtfully and respectfully, offering a reasoned defense of the hope within us (1 Pet. 3:15).

Peter reassures us of God's unfailing love and his promise to one day bring us home when Yeshua returns to establish his kingdom on earth. This is the hope that enables us to "rejoice with joy that is inexpressible and filled with glory" (1 Pet. 1:8), even in the midst of suffering and persecution. Though society may slander and reject us, Peter reminds us that we are never rejected by God. In his opening greeting, he refers to us as God's "elect." He has chosen us and sanctified us. We have a secure identity, a spiritual family, and a God-given purpose.

Chapter 2

An Everlasting Inheritance
(1 Peter 1:3–12)

3 Blessed be the God and Father of our Lord Jesus Christ! According to his great mercy, he has caused us to be born again to a living hope through the resurrection of Jesus Christ from the dead, **4** to an inheritance that is imperishable, undefiled, and unfading, kept in heaven for you, **5** who by God's power are being guarded through faith for a salvation ready to be revealed in the last time. **6** In this you rejoice, though now for a little while, if necessary, you have been grieved by various trials, **7** so that the tested genuineness of your faith—more precious than gold that perishes though it is tested by fire—may be found to result in praise and glory and honor at the revelation of Jesus Christ. **8** Though you have not seen him, you love him. Though you do not now see him, you believe in him and rejoice with joy that is inexpressible and filled with glory, **9** obtaining the outcome of your faith, the salvation of your souls.

10 Concerning this salvation, the prophets who prophesied about the grace that was to be yours searched and inquired carefully, **11** inquiring what person or time the Spirit of Christ in them was indicating when he predicted the sufferings of Christ and the subsequent glories. **12** It was revealed to them that they were serving not themselves but you, in the things that have now been announced to you through those who preached the good news to you by the Holy Spirit sent from heaven, things into which angels long to look.

An Everlasting Inheritance (1 Peter 1:3–12)

In 1 Peter 1:1–2, Peter describes his readers as "resident aliens"—strangers dwelling in a land that is not truly their home. And yet, he also calls them "elect" or "chosen." Their status as strangers is part of God's plan, and the Spirit is actively sanctifying them and leading them toward a life of obedience. He now lifts their eyes from their present challenges to a future reality. In 1 Peter 1:3–12, he speaks of their living hope and the everlasting inheritance that awaits them.

Peter begins the body of his epistle with a blessing: "Blessed be the God and Father of our Lord Jesus Christ" (1 Pet. 1:3). This blessing is presented in the form of a *berakhah*, a traditional Jewish liturgical prayer that often begins with "Blessed be God/the Lord."[1] A *berakhah* simply means "blessing" and serves as an expression of gratitude directed toward God. In Jewish tradition, it became customary to recite *berakhot* on various occasions, even in response to receiving bad news. Many familiar *berakhot*, such as those recited over bread and wine on *Erev Shabbat*,[2] typically begin with the same phrase: *Barukh Atah Adonai Eloheinu Melekh ha-Olam* ("Blessed are You, Lord our God, King of the Universe"). These liturgical prayers have their roots in the synagogue services of Peter's time.[3] Remarkably, Peter includes Yeshua in his *berakhah*: "Blessed be the God and Father *of our Lord Jesus Christ*" (1 Pet. 1:3, emphasis added). He follows the traditional Jewish form of blessing God, yet immediately affirms the Father's relationship with our Lord Yeshua. He then builds the entire blessing around the work of the Messiah.[4] For

---

1   Craig S. Keener, *1 Peter: A Commentary* (Grand Rapids: Baker Academic, 2021), 64.
2   *Erev Shabbat* means "Sabbath evening" and refers to Friday evening, when the observance of the Sabbath begins. It is traditionally accompanied by prayers and a special meal.
3   For example, the *Shemoneh Esrei*, or "Eighteen Benedictions," follows a similar structure. This collection of *berakhot* was an ancient communal prayer regularly recited in the synagogues. Although it wasn't finalized until after the destruction of Jerusalem in 70 A.D., its foundational elements undoubtedly date back to an earlier period. See, e.g., David Instone-Brewer, "The Eighteen Benedictions and the Minim Before 70 CE," *JTS* 54, no. 1 (April 2003), 25–44.
4   Karen H. Jobes, *1 Peter*, BECNT (Grand Rapids: Baker Academic, 2005), 99.

An Everlasting Inheritance (1 Peter 1:3–12)

Peter, the Father and the Son cannot be disassociated from each other—honoring the Father necessarily involves acknowledging the Son (cf. 1 John 2:22–25).

What does Peter mean when he says that God has mercifully caused his readers to be "born again" (1 Pet. 1:3)? Throughout his epistle, Peter uses the imagery of family to describe the believer's relationship with God. Followers of the Messiah are called to live "as obedient children" (1 Pet. 1:14) and to call on God "as Father" (1 Pet. 1:17). By putting their faith in the Messiah and believing "the good news that was preached" to them, Peter's readers have undergone a spiritual "birth" into God's family (1 Pet. 1:23–25). This new birth is made possible "through the resurrection of Jesus Christ from the dead" (1 Pet. 1:3), which is the guarantee that there will be a future resurrection of all believers (cf. 1 Cor. 15:22–23). The new life believers have received will reach its ultimate fulfillment in the coming age when God births an entire new heavens and earth, free of sin, death, and suffering (Matt 24:8; 2 Pet. 3:13; Rev. 21–22).[5] This new birth of believers produces a "living hope." Because God has already fulfilled his promise in raising Yeshua from the dead, believers can confidently place their hope in what God has promised to bring about in the future. As Scot McKnight writes, "It is not so much that believers are now living 'full of hope,' but that they have a fixed 'hope,' a clear vision of what God will do for them in the future."[6]

Those who have been "born again" as God's children have "an inheritance that is imperishable, undefiled, and unfading, kept in heaven for you" (1 Pet. 1:4). What is the believers' inheritance? It is the kingdom

---

5   See Scot McKnight: "The new birth God has given to Peter and his readers, changing their status before God (2:24; 3:18, 21; Titus 3:5) and their lifestyle before others (1 Peter 1:22–23), theologians call regeneration. It is part of the large drama of cosmic regeneration (Matt. 19:28) that finds its climax in the glorious final existence (Rev. 19–22). Thus, through the new creation work of Jesus as a result of his resurrection, the new life the church receives through him is part of that grand act of a new creation" (*1 Peter*, NIVAC [Grand Rapids: Zondervan, 1996], 70).

6   McKnight, *1 Peter*, 70.

An Everlasting Inheritance (1 Peter 1:3–12)

of God (Matt. 25:34; 1 Cor. 15:50) and eternal life (Matt. 19:29; Titus 3:7).[7] This inheritance is imperishable—it will never die or cease to exist. It is undefiled—untouched by the corruption or stain of the world. It is unfading—it will never lose its worth. And finally, it is kept in heaven—securely guarded by God himself, beyond the reach of anyone who might seek to take it away.[8]

Peter continues by describing believers as those "who by God's power are being guarded through faith" (1 Pet. 1:5). Just as God keeps the inheritance secure, his power also currently protects believers. Believers can trust that God will protect them through trials (1 Pet. 1:7), persecution (1 Pet. 3:13–4:19), and spiritual attacks from the devil (1 Pet. 5:8–9). After announcing the great "salvation ready to be revealed in the last time" (1 Pet. 1:5), Peter speaks of the joy that they presently experience as they look ahead to that promised future. He writes, "in this you rejoice." Rejoice in what? In everything he has just described: God's great mercy, their new birth into a living hope, and the assurance of eternal life they have received through the resurrection of the Messiah. Peter's readers rejoice even though they "have been grieved by various trials" (1 Pet. 1:6). In other words, despite present circumstances that may cause fear or sorrow, followers of Yeshua respond with joy. Even when things seem bleak, believers know how the story ends and their living hope prompts them to rejoice.

Additionally (and paradoxically), the trials believers face in the present age serve a good and necessary purpose. Trials test the genuineness of their faith, preparing them to offer unhindered praise when Yeshua returns: "so that the tested genuineness of your faith—more precious than gold that perishes though it is tested by fire—may be found

---

7 Duane F. Watson, "First Peter," in *First and Second Peter*, by Duane F. Watson and Terrance Callan, PCNT (Grand Rapids: Baker Academic, 2012), 24.

8 See Watson, "First Peter," 25: "The passive participle of the verb 'kept' (*tēreō*) refers to God as the one preserving and guarding the inheritance; keeping is another aspect of God's mercy (1:3)."

to result in praise and glory and honor at the revelation of Jesus Christ" (1 Pet. 1:7). To illustrate this, Peter uses the analogy of refining gold with fire. In the ancient world, precious metals like gold were heated to high temperatures to burn away impurities.[9] In the same way, God uses trials to refine his people, purifying their faith like a precious metal. These challenges strengthen their trust in him. As the Psalmist declares, "Before I was afflicted I went astray, but now I keep your word" (Ps. 119:67). Peter teaches that genuine faith is "more precious than gold" in God's eyes.[10] Trials serve to purify that faith, shaping believers into the people God intended them to be for his glory. Like James, Peter sees trials as a means of bringing God's people to maturity (cf. James 1:2–4).

Peter goes on to describe his audience as those who love and believe in the Messiah, even though they don't currently see him: "Though you have not seen him, you love him" (1 Pet. 1:8). Despite not seeing him, they nevertheless "rejoice with joy that is inexpressible and filled with glory" (1 Pet. 1:8). He affirms that they are already experiencing the beginning of the salvation that will be fully revealed at the end of the age (1 Pet. 1:9).[11] Their joy is not based on what they see—the hardships and difficulties of the present—but in the hope they have in the promised salvation. Because they have been born into a living hope, believers can experience a deep and enduring joy, even while they are suffering.

In 1 Peter 1:10–12, Peter explains that the prophets looked ahead to the salvation now experienced by his readers. They foretold the Messiah's suffering and the blessings that would come to believers. The very message the prophets anticipated has now been proclaimed to Peter's audience through those who preached the good news by the Holy Spirit

---

9   Keener, *1 Peter*, 76.
10 According to Paul J. Achtemeier, Peter appears to be making an argument from the lesser to the greater: "if perishable, and hence less valuable, gold must be so tested, how much more must faith, which is imperishable and hence of greater value" (*1 Peter*, Hermeneia [Minneapolis: Fortress Press, 1996], 102).
11 Watson, "First Peter," 27.

(1 Pet. 1:12). These revealed truths are so profound that even angels "are looking down to gain a view, like wedding attendees attempting to steal a glance at the bride before her appearance."[12] Peter's point is clear: his readers stand in a uniquely privileged position, one that surpasses even that of the prophets and angels. The hope and glory now revealed to them is the fulfillment of God's great story of redemption.

Lessons for Today: Hope in the Midst of Trials

As we have studied this section of Peter's epistle, we have been reflecting on the hope we have as followers of Yeshua. According to Peter, it is a hope that fills us with inexpressible joy—a joy that transcends our present circumstances and is not dependent upon the ups and downs of this life. It is a joy that only those who trust in God can truly possess. Without God, the suffering we face would be meaningless. Without God, our suffering would serve no purpose. Our lives would be full of meaningless misery with no end in sight and no greater good being accomplished. But because we know the glorious truth of the Gospel and how the story ends, we can rejoice in spite of the suffering we experience in the present. As the book of Ecclesiastes reminds us, a day is coming when God will bring every deed into judgment (Eccles. 12:13–14). True justice will be established in the world to come, and it is this hope that fuels how we live before God here and now. We view our present lives through the lens of the age to come.

How often do we find ourselves disheartened by the condition of the world around us? It is easy to feel overwhelmed when we witness the deep corruption in political leadership and the implementation of immoral and destructive policies. It is just as easy to be discouraged as we watch society drift further into wickedness and grow increasingly hostile toward those who follow Yeshua. Even so, we rejoice! Why? Because our hope is not found in

---

12 McKnight, *1 Peter*, 73.

political leaders or the temporary circumstances of this world. No matter what we see happening around us, we hold onto hope because a greater kingdom is coming. Evil will not prevail. God will set all things right in the end.

On a more personal level, when we go through seasons of loss or face struggles in our relationships—especially when those we care about deeply hurt or abandon us—it is easy to become consumed by the despair of the moment. It is natural to focus only on the pain right in front of us. We may feel like giving up—on morality, on God, even on life itself. But as believers, we are called to live in light of the age to come. We understand that beyond our present trials, there is hope for a glorious future.

In the meantime, the trials we now face are actually for our good. They are not there to weaken us and wear us down; on the contrary, they are a tool God uses to refine and strengthen our faith. God prioritizes our character over our comfort. Therefore, as we walk through difficulties, we can turn to him and pray, "Lord, what are you teaching me through this? Show me anything in my life that may be holding me back from becoming who you created me to be!"

Be encouraged, as you have been born again to a living hope. This present trial is not the end of the story and will soon be eclipsed by the glory of the coming kingdom, an inheritance secured for you through the Messiah's resurrection. God is using this time, and the hardship and misery it contains, to prepare you for that day.

Chapter 3

Be Holy
(1 Peter 1:13–25)

13 Therefore, preparing your minds for action, and being sober-minded, set your hope fully on the grace that will be brought to you at the revelation of Jesus Christ. **14** As obedient children, do not be conformed to the passions of your former ignorance, **15** but as he who called you is holy, you also be holy in all your conduct, **16** since it is written, "You shall be holy, for I am holy." **17** And if you call on him as Father who judges impartially according to each one's deeds, conduct yourselves with fear throughout the time of your exile, **18** knowing that you were ransomed from the futile ways inherited from your forefathers, not with perishable things such as silver or gold, **19** but with the precious blood of Christ, like that of a lamb without blemish or spot. **20** He was foreknown before the foundation of the world but was made manifest in the last times for the sake of you **21** who through him are believers in God, who raised him from the dead and gave him glory, so that your faith and hope are in God.

22 Having purified your souls by your obedience to the truth for a sincere brotherly love, love one another earnestly from a pure heart, **23** since you have been born again, not of perishable seed but of imperishable, through the living and abiding word of God; **24** for "All flesh is like grass and all its glory like the flower of grass. The grass withers, and the flower falls, **25** but the word of the Lord remains forever." And this word is the good news that was preached to you.

Be Holy (1 Peter 1:13–25)

After reflecting on the blessings that have come to those who put their faith in Yeshua (a new identity, a living hope, and the assurance of salvation), Peter now turns to the believer's calling to live differently in response to these blessings. He opens this next section with the word "therefore," indicating that everything he has just said about who his readers are in the Messiah serves as the foundation for the instructions he is about to give them. As Scot McKnight puts it, "Theology prompts ethics."[1]

Peter begins his instructions with an emphasis on the mind. Believers are called to prepare "your minds for action" and be "sober-minded." Rightly focusing your mind is necessary for setting your hope "on the grace that will be brought to you at the revelation of Jesus Christ" (1 Pet. 1:13). The phrase "preparing your minds for action" is more directly translated "girding up the loins of your minds."[2] This imagery comes from the ancient practice of gathering up one's long robe and tucking it into a belt to move freely and act quickly (cf. 1 Kings 18:46). A modern equivalent might be the phrase "roll up your sleeves."[3] Yeshua used this same imagery when teaching about readiness for his return, saying, "Stay dressed for action"—literally, "Let your loins stay girded" (Luke 12:35). Peter applies this metaphor to the mind, urging believers to get their thoughts in order and to mentally prepare for the work God has set before them. The second exhortation builds on the first: be "sober-minded." In other words, Peter says to exercise mental discipline and not get distracted. He wants his readers to keep their minds centered on their mission as disciples of Yeshua.

Why does Peter begin his instructions to believers with a focus on the mind? Why does he stress the importance of right thinking? Because the decision to sin often starts with a feeling or craving (James 1:13–16),

---

[1] Scot McKnight, *1 Peter*, NIVAC (Grand Rapids: Zondervan, 1996), 84.
[2] Craig S. Keener, *1 Peter: A Commentary* (Grand Rapids: Baker Academic, 2021), 92; See also McKnight, 1 Peter, 85.
[3] Duane F. Watson, "First Peter," in *First and Second Peter*, by Duane F. Watson and Terrance Callan, PCNT (Grand Rapids: Baker Academic, 2012), 32

and that is precisely where the devil targets his attacks. The devil operates within the realm of human emotions and desires (Eph. 4:26–27), which is why Peter later warns his readers again, saying, "Be sober-minded; be watchful. Your adversary the devil prowls around like a roaring lion, seeing someone to devour" (1 Pet. 5:8). Although believers may not be able to control their emotions and desires, they can choose to control their thoughts. Consequently, Peter's exhortations to be sober-minded and to prepare the mind are calls to bring their emotions and desires under the direction of righteous thinking. This mental discipline enables them to "resist" the attacks of the devil (1 Pet. 5:9).

Having called believers to get their thoughts in order and set their hope fully on the grace to come, Peter now continues by urging them to respond to that hope with lives that reflect God's holiness:

> As obedient children, do not be conformed to the passions of your former ignorance, but as he who called you is holy, you also be holy in all your conduct, since it is written, "You shall be holy, for I am holy."
> —1 Peter 1:14–16

The salvation believers have received through their faith in Yeshua is intended to lead to a life of holiness. This reflects the consistent biblical pattern: God first grants salvation, then calls his people to faithful obedience for his glory. The same pattern is seen with Israel: God saved them from slavery in Egypt and then gave them the Torah so they could serve him as a holy people and be a light to the nations (Deut. 4:5–8). With the gift of salvation comes the responsibility to love God and to be holy. As noted in the Introduction, Peter's original audience consists mostly of Gentile believers. Here, he urges these Gentile believers to no longer conform to the passions and lifestyle they once followed in ignorance. Instead, having been born again into God's family, like Israel, they are now called to live as God's "obedient children," which means being holy:

Be Holy (1 Peter 1:13–25)

"just as he who called you is holy, so be holy in all your conduct" (1 Pet. 1:15).

What does it mean to "be holy"? Conceptually, to "be holy" means to be separate from what is common or secular and dedicated to what is sacred.[4] For instance, after he finished creating the universe, God made the seventh day—the Sabbath—"holy" by setting it apart from the other days and dedicating it to a sacred purpose (Gen. 2:1–3). Similarly, God called Israel out from among the nations, separating them for himself so they would become a "holy nation" (Exod. 19:6; cf. 1 Pet. 2:9). The same principle applies to the priests and Levites within Israel; they were set apart from the rest of the people and dedicated to serving in the tabernacle (2 Chron. 23:6). This principle is consistent throughout Scripture. Here, Peter instructs believers to be holy in all their "conduct," meaning their lives should be set apart from the secular and dedicated to the sacred. Why are believers called to be holy? Because "he who called you is holy." God is perfectly holy and expects his "obedient children" to reflect his nature, including his holiness.[5]

What does "holy conduct" look like practically? Peter directs his readers to Scripture for the answer. He introduces the command "You shall be holy, for I am holy" with "it is written," and then he quotes Leviticus (Lev. 11:44; 19:2). This means that Peter considers Leviticus to be a guide for defining holy conduct. As Richard Sabuin writes, "Peter does not merely borrow the conventional expression without a consideration of its context, rather he must have thought the ways to become holy were written in Leviticus."[6] In the context of Leviticus, the passages contain-

---

4   BDAG (9-10) defines "holy" (ἅγιος) as "pert. to being dedicated or consecrated to the service of God." For the Hebrew equivalent (קָדֹשׁ), see Thomas E. McComiskey: "The adjective *qadosh* (holy) denominates that which is intrinsically sacred or which has been admitted to the sphere of the sacred by divine rite or cultic act. It connotes that which is distinct from the common or profane" (קָדַשׁ in TWOT, 788).

5   See Keener, *1 Peter*, 100: "Children (1:14) typically behave like their fathers; those who invoke God as Father (1:17) should follow his ways (1:15¬-16)."

6   Richard Sabuin, "Sabbath in the General Epistles," in *The Sabbath in the New Testament*

ing the command to be holy are connected to various laws that outline how God's people are to live. For example, Leviticus 19:2 says, "You shall be holy, for I the LORD your God am holy," followed by detailed instructions on what holiness looks like in practice. The chapter goes on to command honor for one's parents, observance of God's Sabbaths (Lev. 19:3), rejection of idolatry (Lev. 19:4), and care for the poor (Lev. 19:9–10). Holiness also includes personal integrity, such as refraining from lying, stealing, or defrauding others (Lev. 19:11–14). It involves upholding justice in court and avoiding hatred, slander, and revenge (Lev. 19:15–17). Leviticus also commands, "You shall love your neighbor as yourself" (Lev. 19:18), which Yeshua calls the second greatest commandment in the Torah (Matt. 22:37–40). These practical expressions of obedience in Leviticus are what Peter has in mind when he calls believers to be holy. Indeed, throughout his epistle, Peter exhorts his readers to do many things that are specifically commanded in Leviticus.[7]

Peter continues by exhorting his readers, who call on God "as Father," to conduct themselves with "fear" during their time as resident aliens in this world (1 Pet. 1:17). Why must believers live with reverent fear? Because God is the judge of both the living and the dead (1 Pet. 4:5), and his judgment begins with his own household (1 Pet. 4:17). Knowing that God "judges impartially according to each one's deeds" (1 Pet. 1:17), believers are to walk in awe and reverence before him. He is utterly holy and expects his children to be holy as well. Craig S. Keener puts it well:

---

and in Theology: Implications for Christians in the Twenty-First Century, ed. Ekkehardt Mueller and Eike Mueller (Silver Spring, MD: Biblical Research Institute, 2023), 223.

7   For instance, several of the behaviors that Peter instructs his readers to "put away" in 1 Peter 2:1—such as malice, deceit, and slander—are also prohibited in Leviticus 19:11–18. His warning in 1 Peter 4:3–4 to avoid pagan practices echoes the commands found in Leviticus 18:1–3, 24–30 and 20:23. Moreover, Peter's exhortation to honor elders reflects the command in Leviticus 19:32.

Be Holy (1 Peter 1:13–25)

> In this context (cf. 1:13), such reverence entails always keeping in mind the future judgment, behaving always in the recognition that God the just judge takes account of all of one's behavior. Certainly many people who claim to be Christians would spend their time and resources differently if they lived their daily lives cognizant of God's presence and values.[8]

Peter now turns his focus to how the Messiah's blood has ransomed his readers from the futile way of life they once lived before knowing God (1 Pet. 1:18). Like a sacrificial offering,[9] Yeshua gave his life to deliver them from the power of sin and death (1 Pet. 1:19). Peter compares Yeshua to a lamb without blemish or defect, highlighting his sinlessness (1 Pet. 2:22; cf. Heb. 4:15). While all have sinned and fall short of God's glory (Rom. 3:23) and are deserving of death, Yeshua, though innocent, died in place of the guilty so they might be spared the judgment they deserve. Peter adds that Yeshua "was foreknown before the foundation of the world" (1 Pet. 1:20), meaning that God's plan of salvation through the Messiah's death and resurrection was already ordained long before creation. And now, "in the last times," the Messiah has been revealed in human history to bring that plan to completion "for the sake of you." That is, God raised Yeshua from the dead "so that your faith and hope are in God" (1 Pet. 1:21). The foundation of the believer's faith and hope is found in the Messiah's resurrection. Just as the Messiah rose to new life out of death, so believers have been born into a new life out of their old sinful existence.

Peter concludes this section by urging his readers to "love one another earnestly from a pure heart" (1 Pet. 1:22; cf. John 13:34–35). This again

---

8 Keener, *1 Peter*, 99.
9 See Watson, "First Peter," 35: "Christ is like an unblemished and spotless lamb (1:19b), thus worthy of sacrifice to God; this is a general image drawn from the sacrificial cult of Israel, where only perfect animals could be sacrificed (Exod. 29:1; Lev. 22:17–25; Num. 28–29)."

hearkens back to Leviticus: "you shall love your neighbor as yourself" (Lev. 19:18). But Peter also grounds this command in the reality that God has given them new life. Through the Messiah, they have been "born again." They are no longer the people they once were before knowing him (1 Pet. 1:23). They are now a new people: God's obedient children. To emphasize this, Peter quotes from Isaiah 40:6–8, which contrasts the fleeting nature of human life with the enduring power of God's word (1 Pet. 1:24–25). This eternal word has been planted like a seed in the hearts of believers, producing eternal life. That seed—"the living and abiding word of God"—is the "good news," the Gospel, that was proclaimed to Peter's readers (1 Pet. 1:25). The old sinful life was a temporary thing; the believer's new life of holiness and obedience to God's word is eternal.

Lessons for Today: What Does Holiness Look Like?

What lessons can we draw from this section of Peter's epistle? Two key points stand out.

First, Peter urges his readers to prepare their minds and remain sober-minded. In other words, we must take control of our thoughts. Instead of being led by our emotions, we are to *lead* our emotions with intentional mental discipline. This involves recognizing our own weaknesses and being "watchful," knowing that the enemy is looking for opportunities to prey on those weaknesses (1 Pet. 5:8–9). On a practical level, this may involve setting clear boundaries in areas where we know we are vulnerable. For instance, if you struggle with sexual temptation, it might be wise to avoid using the internet during times when you are feeling lonely, discouraged, or stressed—those moments when you are more likely to be tempted to seek comfort in harmful ways, such as viewing pornography. Putting these kinds of boundaries in place is a way of practicing mental discipline and self-control. Do not give the enemy an opportunity to exploit your weaknesses. Stay focused. And what should that focus be on? Peter says to "set

Be Holy (1 Peter 1:13–25)

your hope fully on the grace that will be brought to you at the revelation of Jesus Christ." In other words, fix your eyes on the finish line. Do not stray to the right or the left, but keep pushing forward, running the race to win (cf. 1 Cor. 9:24–27). The inheritance that awaits is far greater than anything this world can offer.

Second, Peter calls on believers to "be holy," appealing to Leviticus as the guide for what holiness should look like. Generally, most Christians agree with many of the commands in Leviticus mentioned above, such as honoring our parents, caring for the poor, and loving our neighbor. While we may not always live up to these standards, there is broad agreement among Christians that we should strive toward keeping these laws. However, other aspects of holy conduct mentioned in Leviticus are not accepted by many Christians today. For example, the command to "keep my Sabbaths" appears immediately after the call to "be holy" (Lev. 19:2–3). Yet many Christians view the command to observe the seventh-day Sabbath as no longer applicable.[10] If Peter gets his definition of holy conduct from Leviticus, should we not consider Sabbath observance to be part of that holy conduct?

Another place where the command "You shall be holy, for I am holy" appears is in Leviticus 11:44. This verse comes after a list of dietary instructions that outline which animals are considered "clean" and permissible to eat, and which are "unclean" and must not be eaten. This suggests that being holy in all our conduct includes holiness even in dietary choices. Once again, Peter is quoting directly from these passages

---

10   For a detailed study on the relevance of the Sabbath for today, see David Wilber, "A New Testament Case for Christian Sabbath Observance," in *An Introduction to Pronomianism: Essays on One Torah Theology in Modern Christianity* (Jefferson, NC: McFarland & Company, forthcoming). See also David Wilber, "Sabbath Observance in Luke-Acts: Situating the Earliest Followers of Jesus within Judaism," *E-Journal of Religious and Theological Studies* 11, no. 3 (2025), 51–59; David Wilber, *Remember the Sabbath: What the New Testament Says About Sabbath Observance for Christians* (Clover, SC: Pronomian Publishing, 2022).

in Leviticus where holy conduct is clearly defined, and his understanding of holiness is rooted in these very Scriptures.

What does this mean for followers of Yeshua today? It means that if we truly want to follow Peter's instruction to be holy in all our conduct, we should look to the commandments in Leviticus that define what holiness looks like. This includes commandments like honoring parents and caring for the poor, but it also includes practices such as observing the Sabbath and following biblical food laws. If we allow the Bible to define holiness, then all of these practices are part of what it means to be holy.

Admittedly, my view that both Jewish and Gentile followers of Yeshua should observe commandments such as the Sabbath and food laws is a minority position within broader Christianity, and even some within Messianic Judaism may disagree (at least regarding whether *Gentile* believers should observe them). Nevertheless, Yeshua clearly taught that nothing in the Law of Moses would pass away as long as heaven and earth exist, and he urged his followers to keep "even the least" of the commandments (Matt. 5:18–19).[11] He later instructed his disciples to teach the nations "to observe all that I have commanded you" (Matt. 28:20), which would naturally include his earlier words in Matthew 5:19.[12] Since the Sabbath and food laws are part of the Law of Moses, Matthew 28:20 indicates that Yeshua expects Gentiles who

---

11 For a detailed study of this passage, see David Wilber, *How Jesus Fulfilled the Law: A Pronomian Pocket Guide to Matthew 5:17–20* (Clover, SC: Pronomian Publishing, 2024).

12 Some might argue that Matthew 5:19 is not strictly a "command" but rather an exhortation, and therefore should not be counted among the "commands" that Yeshua expects his disciples to teach the Gentiles in Matthew 28:28. However, see Oliver Marjot: "[G]iven its prominent, programmatic place near the beginning of the Sermon on the Mount, there needs to be a compelling reason not to apply Matthew's rhetorical and theological commitment to Torah-observance to Jesus' future Gentile disciples as well as the Jewish ones he addresses within the Gospel's narrative; such a reason is, it seems to me, lacking in the text" ("Israel, Torah and Christ in Matthew and Romans: A Conversation 'within Judaism'" [Ph.D. diss., St Catharine's College, 2022], 82).

Be Holy (1 Peter 1:13–25)

become his disciples to keep these commandments as well.[13] Are the instructions in 1 Peter 1:14–16 an example of Peter carrying out Yeshua's call to teach the Gentiles to observe all that he commanded, including his exhortation to obey "even the least" of the Torah's commandments?

In any case, Peter's message is clear: holiness touches every part of our lives—what we think, how we live, when we rest, and even what we eat. We are called to be sober-minded, guarding our thoughts and desires, because that is where the battle often begins. But holiness is about more than just avoiding sin; it is about being dedicated to God in every area of life. Just as Peter draws on Leviticus to define holy conduct, we should take the same Scriptures seriously. If we truly want to live as obedient children, reflecting the character of our holy Father, then our mindset, our lifestyle, and our daily habits must all be shaped by his word.

---

13 Daniel J. Harrington has made a similar argument: "There is no indication that Matthew expected these Gentiles to convert to Judaism formally and to be circumcised. But it is possible in view of Mt. 5.17-19 that he did expect them to observe the Mosaic Law, at least as it was interpreted by Jesus. That observance may well have entailed the Biblical rules pertaining to sabbath rest, forbidden foods and ritual purity" ("Matthew and Paul" in *Matthew and His Christian Contemporaries*, ed. David C. Sim and Boris Repshinski [New York: T&T Clark, 2008], 18). See also Marjot, "Israel, Torah and Christ," 82; Matthias Konradt, *The Gospel according to Matthew: A Commentary*, trans. M. Eugene Boring (Waco, TX: Baylor University Press, 2020), 446; Anders Runesson, *Divine Wrath and Salvation in Matthew: The Narrative World of the First Gospel* (Minneapolis: Fortress Press, 2016), 350n16.

Chapter 4

You Are God's People
(1 Peter 2:1–10)

> **1** So put away all malice and all deceit and hypocrisy and envy and all slander. **2** Like newborn infants, long for the pure spiritual milk, that by it you may grow up into salvation—**3** if indeed you have tasted that the Lord is good. **4** As you come to him, a living stone rejected by men but in the sight of God chosen and precious, **5** you yourselves like living stones are being built up as a spiritual house, to be a holy priesthood, to offer spiritual sacrifices acceptable to God through Jesus Christ. **6** For it stands in Scripture: "Behold, I am laying in Zion a stone, a cornerstone chosen and precious, and whoever believes in him will not be put to shame." **7** So the honor is for you who believe, but for those who do not believe, "The stone that the builders rejected has become the cornerstone," **8** and "A stone of stumbling, and a rock of offense." They stumble because they disobey the word, as they were destined to do. **9** But you are a chosen race, a royal priesthood, a holy nation, a people for his own possession, that you may proclaim the excellencies of him who called you out of darkness into his marvelous light. **10** Once you were not a people, but now you are God's people; once you had not received mercy, but now you have received mercy.

In chapter 1 of his epistle, Peter explained that believers have received a new identity and are therefore called to be holy just as God is holy. By embracing the "good news that was preached" to them, Peter declares that his readers have been "born again" as obedient children of God (1 Pet.

You Are God's People (1 Peter 2:1–10)

1:23–25). Now, in 1 Peter 2:1–10, he continues by urging his readers to grow in their new life and to understand their role as a chosen people.

Peter begins this section by calling his readers to "put away all malice and all deceit and hypocrisy and envy and all slander" (1 Pet. 2:1). These attitudes and behaviors are inconsistent with their new identity in the Messiah and stand in direct opposition to the command to "love one another earnestly from a pure heart" (1 Pet. 1:22). Paul J. Achtemeier provides an excellent summary of why Peter lists these particular vices:

> κακία ["malice"] is surely a power that destroys community, and is identified as directly opposed to acts motivated from love in Rom 13:10. The next set of three vices—deception, hypocrisy, envy—are also inimical to a community based on mutual love, since deception and hypocrisy point to acts intended to serve the individual at the expense of the neighbor, and envy means to wish better for oneself than for the other…In this context, the final vice (καταλαλιά, "evil speech") probably refers to habitual disparagement of others rather than some kind of openly slanderous speech. Taken together, they represent the kind of attitudes and actions in whose presence true community based on love is impossible, and that are therefore absent among those who have heeded the command to love one another.[1]

Since believers have become part of God's family, they are called to love their fellow brothers and sisters. This means they must put away any attitudes or behaviors that damage the unity and health of the family. The verb "put away" (ἀποτίθημι) is used metaphorically, evoking the image of taking off a garment.[2] Believers are to "take off" their former

---

1 Paul J. Achtemeier, *1 Peter*, Hermeneia (Minneapolis: Fortress Press, 1996), 144–145.
2 Duane F. Watson, "First Peter," in *First and Second Peter*, by Duane F. Watson and Terrance Callan, PCNT (Grand Rapids: Baker Academic, 2012), 43; Craig Keener, *1 Peter: A Commentary* (Grand Rapids: Baker Academic, 2021), 120.

You Are God's People (1 Peter 2:1–10)

behaviors and dress themselves in a new way of life marked by holiness. As the apostle Paul similarly writes, "So then let us cast off the works of darkness and put on the armor of light" (Rom. 13:12).

Peter further exhorts his readers to "long for the pure spiritual milk" like "newborn infants" (1 Pet. 2:2). Just as a newborn relies on his mother's milk for physical growth, believers depend on God's "milk" for spiritual growth.[3] This "pure spiritual milk" refers to God's word (1 Pet. 1:25). The same word that brought about their new birth (1 Pet. 1:23–25) now provides their spiritual sustenance.[4] It is this same life-giving word that believers must continually desire in order to mature and grow into the fullness of their salvation.[5] Having "tasted that the Lord is good" (1 Pet. 2:3; cf. Ps. 34:8), Peter invites his readers to pursue a deeper, ongoing experience of that goodness.[6]

The believer's desire for spiritual sustenance draws them closer to the Messiah, whom Peter describes as "a living stone rejected by men but in the sight of God chosen and previous" (1 Pet. 2:4). Here, Peter draws a parallel between the Messiah and his followers: just as the Messiah was rejected by people, so too are believers; and just as the Messiah is chosen and precious to God, so are they (1 Pet. 1:1, 15; 2:9). Moreover, as the Messiah was vindicated through his resurrection, believers will also be vindicated at the end of the age when they are raised to eternal life (1 Pet. 1:3–9). In the meantime, however, they are called to share in the Messiah's sufferings (1 Pet. 2:24; 4:13–16).

---

3   Keener, *1 Peter*, 123.
4   Achtemeier, *1 Peter*, 147.
5   Elsewhere in the New Testament, "milk" is used as a metaphor for basic teachings meant for new believers (Heb. 5:12–14). However, that does not appear to be Peter's intended meaning here since he depicts this "milk" as being something that all believers should continually desire. As Achtemeier (*1 Peter*, 146) writes, "The point here is not that the readers are to advance beyond the stage of being immature Christians; rather the point is that their desire for such milk is to be as constant and unrelenting as the infant's desire for its milk."
6   Watson, "First Peter," 45.

You Are God's People (1 Peter 2:1–10)

As believers "come to him," they are being built into a spiritual house: "you yourselves like living stones are being built up as a spiritual house, to be a holy priesthood, to offer spiritual sacrifices acceptable to God through Jesus Christ" (1 Pet. 2:4–5). Paul uses this same imagery to depict the unified community of Jews and Gentiles in the Messiah (Eph. 2:19–22; 1 Cor. 3:16–17). Here, Peter emphasizes both the believer's connection to the Messiah as well as their connection to each other. As Scot McKnight observes:

> The churches in Asia Minor must see themselves as "living stones," connected to the "living Stone" (2:4), and they must unify themselves (1:22–2:3) so that they may become a spiritual house. That is, instead of being a simple group of social outcasts, they must find their identity and cohesion in their spiritual relationship to the living Stone.[7]

As believers "come to him," they are being built into a spiritual house: "you yourselves like living stones are being built up as a spiritual house, to be a holy priesthood, to offer spiritual sacrifices acceptable to Before we continue, we need to address a common misunderstanding. Peter's statements about his readers being built into a "spiritual house" and serving as "a holy priesthood" that offers "spiritual sacrifices" (1 Pet. 2:5, 9) are frequently interpreted as teaching supersessionism. That is, many claim that Peter presents "the church" as having replaced Israel, the Levitical priesthood, and the temple. For instance, R. L. Solberg explicitly claims that Yeshua "supersedes the Law and its Levitical priesthood."[8] Based on this assumption, he interprets 1 Peter 2:4–5 to mean that "those

---

7   Scot McKnight, *1 Peter*, NIVAC (Grand Rapids: Zondervan, 1996), 106.
8   R. L. Solberg, *Torahism: Are Christians Required to Keep the Law of Moses?* 2nd ed. (Franklin, TN: Williamson College Press, 2022), 260, Kindle edition.

in Christ" now constitute "the priesthood of the New Covenant under Jesus," which he sees as incompatible with "the priestly Mosaic laws."[9]

However, while the idea that the church has replaced the temple and priesthood is often *read into* 1 Peter 2:5, where does the text itself actually make that claim? Apart from certain supersessionist assumptions, the text simply does not demand such a conclusion. As Kelly D. Liebengood writes, "temple imagery...does not necessarily entail a zero-sum game. That is, it is possible to promote community-as-temple imagery without at the same time replacing the Jerusalem temple and its sacrifices."[10] Indeed, the use of such temple imagery was not unique to the apostles. For example, the Pharisees viewed themselves as a priestly group and sought to adapt certain temple practices for use within their own communities,[11] but obviously the Pharisees did not teach that their communities had superseded the Jerusalem temple or its priesthood. As Oskar Skarsaune writes, "Their aim was to extend the sanctity of the temple, not to replace it or make it unnecessary."[12] Similarly, the Qumran community described themselves as "a temple for Israel" and "a perfect and true house in Israel," which offered sacrifices of praise and prayer (C.D. 11.21; 1QS 8.5–9; 10.6).[13] Still, despite using such imagery for their sect, they were not claiming to have superseded the Jerusalem temple or priesthood. Certainty, the Qumran community was critical of the priesthood of their day, but they still sent votive offerings to the Jerusalem temple and looked forward to its purification and restoration in the future.[14]

---

9 Solberg, *Torahism*, 266–267, Kindle edition.
10 Kelly D. Liebengood, *Reading 1 Peter After Supersessionism: Jewish Apostolic Affirmation of Gentile Israelhood* (Eugene, OR: Cascade, 2025), 135.
11 Oskar Skarsaune, *In the Shadow of the Temple: Jewish Influences on Early Christianity* (Downers Grove, IL: IVP Academic, 2002), 117–122.
12 Skarsaune, *In the Shadow*, 121.
13 See Keener, *1 Peter*, 129–131.
14 See Skarsaune, *In the Shadow*, 114–115: "Since the days of the 'wicked priest,' the Essenes regarded the temple as polluted and the sacrifices as invalid. Nevertheless they continued

You Are God's People (1 Peter 2:1–10)

Like these other Jewish sects of his time, Peter describes his community as a spiritual temple and priesthood without suggesting that his community has superseded the temple or priesthood in Jerusalem. This fact is evident in the Book of Acts, where Luke depicts Peter and the other apostles worshiping at the Jerusalem temple "every day" (Acts 2:46; 5:42; cf. Luke 24:53). Luke also notes that Peter and John went to the temple during the "hour of prayer" (Acts 3:1), a reference to one of the designated times for corporate prayer that corresponded to the daily sacrificial offerings (cf. Exod. 29:39–41; Num. 28:4; Ezra 9:4; Josephus, Antiquities 14.65).[15] Paul also participated in temple worship and presented offerings (Acts 21:17–26; cf. 24:17). Thus, according to Acts, Peter continued to take part in the Jerusalem temple services even while teaching that followers of the Messiah are a spiritual temple and priesthood, so he did not view one as superseding or canceling out the other.

Just as temple imagery was common within the broader Jewish world in Peter's time, so too was the idea of offering "spiritual sacrifices." The Wisdom of Sirach, written around 180 BCE, describes obedience to the Torah and generosity toward the poor as types of offerings (Sirach 35:1–5). First-century Jewish teacher Philo wrote that "piety" is a "real

---

to send votive offerings to the temple, and their rejection of the present temple service was by no means meant as a disparagement of the temple or a declaration that its service was insignificant. To the contrary, they rejected the present polluted service precisely because they valued the temple so much. In fact, they expected to take control of the temple and either cleanse it from pollution or rebuild it in the near future, when the great eschatological war had begun. The spiritual worship and the community meal at Qumran were only temporary substitutes for the temple service, which was to be resumed as soon as possible." See also Liebengood, *Reading 1 Peter After Supersessionism*, 132-133: "the Qumran community did not see itself as the 'new' and 'true' temple that offers legitimate and effective sacrifices in the place of the Jerusalem temple. Instead, at best, these sectarians at Qumran saw their community a provisional response to an undesired circumstance, namely the ritually and morally defiled temple."

15 Craig S. Keener, *Acts: An Exegetical Commentary, Volume 2: 3:1-14:28* (Grand Rapids: Baker Academic, 2013), 1044-1047).

and true sacrifice" (Philo, *On the Life of Moses* 2.108).[16] The Hebrew Scriptures themselves similarly speak of contrition and prayer as sacrificial offerings (Pss. 51:16–19; 141:2). When Peter refers to his readers as those who "offer spiritual sacrifices," he is calling them to be a community engaged in repentance, praise, good works, and care for one another (1 Pet. 1:15–16; 2:24; 3:6, 10–13). Such sacrifices are "acceptable to God through Jesus Christ" (1 Pet. 2:5).

In 1 Peter 2:6, Peter supports his claim that Yeshua is "a living stone" by quoting Isaiah 28:16. Peter presents Yeshua as the "cornerstone" that God declared he would lay in Zion. Peter identifies his readers as those who "believe" in this stone and who therefore "will not be put to shame." As Watson writes, "The recipients can be assured that however they are shamed by their neighbors for association with the rejected Stone (v. 7), they will not be shamed by God."[17] In contrast, "those who do not believe" have rejected the very stone that God has honored as the cornerstone, and they stumble over him (1 Pet. 2:7–8; cf. Ps. 118:22; Isa. 8:14). Peter adds, "They stumble because they disobey the word, as they were destined to do" (1 Pet. 2:8). The "word" specifically refers to "the good news that was preached" (1 Pet. 1:25), and they "disobey" this word because they "do not believe" (1 Pet. 2:7).[18]

But what does Peter mean when he says, "as they were destined to do?" Does this mean that God *predestined* certain people to stumble and disobey? Did God decide ahead of time who would believe and who would reject him? Such a reading seems to contradict other passages of Scripture that clearly affirm that God's desire is that nobody should perish but that *all* would repent and come to the knowledge of the truth (2 Pet. 3:9; 1 Tim. 2:4). Scripture shows that God genuinely wants people to repent and is grieved when they do not: "I have no pleasure in the death of the wicked, but that the wicked turn from his way and live" (Ezek.

---

16 For more early Jewish sources on "spiritual sacrifices," see Keener, *1 Peter*, 130–132.
17 Watson, "First Peter," 50.
18 Watson, "First Peter," 50.

33:11). If God predestined their unbelief, why would he grieve their disobedience and express a desire for their obedience if it was his will for them to disobey all along? A more biblically consistent interpretation is that Peter is not claiming that God predestined certain people to reject him but rather that God has predetermined *the punishment* for those who persist in unbelief. Armin J. Panning puts this point well:

> What is it that has been determined (ἐτέθησαν)? The Scriptures make it very plain that there is an inseparable connection between unbelief and the punishment for unbelief. In the case of unbelievers there invariably is a "stumbling" and a "falling" that leads to eternal death. However, what has been determined is not that some should be unbelievers, but that their unbelief will be punished. God will not be mocked (Gal 6:7). At his ascension the risen and triumphant Christ not only said, "Whoever believes and is baptized will be saved," but he added the dreadful and the inevitable corollary, "Whoever does not believe will be condemned" (Mark 16:16). Neither of those statements brook any exception. Both have been "set."[19]

Peter does not state that God predestines certain individuals to disobey the word. Rather, he explains that people will respond differently to the Messiah, the "stone." Believers see Yeshua as the precious cornerstone (1 Pet. 2:6–7a) and build their lives upon him, and as a result, they will receive honor. Unbelievers, on the other hand, see him as a "rock of offense" and stumble over him (1 Peter 2:7b–8), leading to their condemnation. God has appointed honor and salvation for those who believe in him, and punishment for those who reject him. Accord-

---

19 Armin J. Panning, "What Has Been Determined (ἐτέθησαν) in 1 Peter 2:8?" *WLQ* 98 (2001), 50.

ing to this view, it is not their unbelief that is predestined, but rather the consequence of that unbelief.

Peter goes on to describe his readers as "a chosen race, a royal priesthood, a holy nation, a people for his own possession" (1 Pet. 2:9), which is language originally used in the Torah to refer to Israel (Exod. 19:5–6; Deut. 7:6; 14:2). Considering that Peter's audience consists mostly of Gentiles (see "Recipients" in the Introduction), his use of this language is striking. Importantly, Peter is not suggesting that the Gentile believers among his readers have superseded Israel. Rather, through Israel's Messiah, they have been brought into the commonwealth of Israel (cf. Eph. 2:11–22). Israel has not been *replaced* but rather *expanded* to include people from the nations who have been "born again" into the family of the God of Israel through the resurrection of Israel's Messiah (1 Pet. 1:3, 23).[20] And just as Israel was always meant to do (cf. Isa. 43:21), Peter calls his readers to "proclaim the excellencies of him who called you out of darkness into his marvelous light" (1 Pet. 1:9). The imagery of light and darkness is a familiar theme in the Hebrew Scriptures—darkness symbolizing separation from God, and light representing his presence (Prov. 2:13; Ps. 43:3; Isa. 2:5; 9:2). In Greek, the term ἐξαγγέλλω ("proclaim") is often used in the Septuagint "for proclaiming the praises and works of God in worship"[21] (Pss. 9:14; 71:15; 107:22). Believers were brought into God's light to glorify him and announce his mighty works to the world (1 Pet. 4:11, 16).

In 1 Peter 2:10, Peter writes, "Once you were not a people, but now you are God's people; once you had not received mercy, but now you have

---

20 See Liebengood, *Reading 1 Peter*, 212: "God's ongoing fidelity to Israel is assumed and therefore unquestioned. What *is* in question, however, is whether and how gentiles fit into what the God of Israel is doing through Israel's Messiah...Peter extends a form of Jewish ethnic identity to his gentile addressees: they also belong to the people of the God of Israel, and this reality is so profound that it requires that they subordinate their inherited gentile identity to Israelhood."
21 Watson, "First Peter," 51. See also Keener, *1 Peter*, 140.

You Are God's People (1 Peter 2:1–10)

received mercy." Here, Peter draws from Hosea 1:10 and 2:23, which prophetically announce a reversal of God's judgment against the northern kingdom of Israel (also called Ephraim). In Hosea, God instructs the prophet to name his second and third children "Not My People" and "No Mercy," symbolizing Israel's estrangement from him (Hosea 1:6–9). As a result of that estrangement, the northern kingdom was exiled and scattered among the nations. Unlike the southern kingdom of Judah, which was later restored from Babylonian exile, much of the northern kingdom did not return.[22] So, when Peter quotes from Hosea, he is alluding to God's promise to restore *all* Israel in the last days. This promise includes the eventual reunion of the faithful remnants from both the northern and southern kingdoms. Like Paul in Romans 9:24–26, Peter applies these restoration prophecies about the northern kingdom of Israel to his *Gentile* readers. In other words, Peter views the inclusion of these faithful Gentiles as a fulfillment of Hosea's prophecy regarding the northern kingdom's restoration.

But how does Peter draw this connection? What do these prophecies about the restoration of Israel have to do with Gentiles? When the northern kingdom of Israel was exiled, they were labeled "not my people." Similarly, Gentiles are, by definition, also "not my people." Through their dispersion among the nations, the northern tribes became so integrated with the Gentiles that they were, to some extent, indistinguishable from them. In Peter's view, then, these Gentiles coming to faith—those once considered "not my people"—are part of the fulfillment of God's promise to restore Israel. Since the northern kingdom had become largely indistinguishable from the nations, the only way for God to restore them was to open the door to *all* the nations. To be clear, Peter is not saying that the Gentiles coming to faith in the Messiah are physical descendants

---

[22] It should be noted that some northern Israelites must have returned with the southern remnant. Luke mentions Anna, a Hebrew prophetess "of the tribe of Asher," who was praising God in Herod's Temple (Luke 2:36).

of ancient Israelites.[23] Rather, he is drawing a connection between the northern kingdom of Israel being called "not my people" and the Gentiles, who also fall under that designation. Because the northern kingdom became "not my people," the path to their restoration necessarily involves bringing in *all* "not my people" (Gentiles). In other words, God's promise to restore Israel has opened the door for all Gentiles to share in that restoration. Jason A. Staples explains it well:

> God has provided for the salvation of the Gentiles by scattering Ephraim among the nations only to be restored. In saving Ephraim, God saves the nations; in saving the nations, God saves Ephraim. Thus, the new covenant not only restores Israel but also—in the unforeseen plan of God—fulfills the promises to Abraham that all the nations would be blessed, not "through" his seed (i.e., as outsiders) but by inclusion and incorporation *in* his seed (Gal 3:8).[24]

If Peter's largely Gentile audience had any lingering uncertainty about their identity in the Messiah, his announcement that they are indeed "a chosen race, a royal priesthood, a holy nation, a people for his own possession" and "God's people" would have left no doubt. According to Peter, those who place their faith in the Messiah belong to God's people. They are members of God's family and his treasured possession.

---

23 For a helpful work that counters the popular idea that modern Gentile believers are physical descendants of the "lost tribes," see J. K. McKee, *Israel in Future Prophecy: Is There a Larger Restoration of the Kingdom of Israel?* (McKinney, TX: Messianic Apologetics, 2013), particularly the chapters dealing with "Two-House Teaching."
24 Jason A. Staples, "What Do the Gentiles have to Do with 'All Israel'? A Fresh Look at Romans 11:25-27," *JBL* 130, no. 2 (2011), 382. See also Jason A. Staples, *Paul and the Resurrection of Israel: Jews, Former Gentiles, Israelites* (New York: Cambridge University Press, 2024); Jason A. Staples, *The Idea of Israel in Second Temple Judaism: A New Theory of People, Exile, and Israelite Identity* (New York: Cambridge University Press, 2021).

You Are God's People (1 Peter 2:1–10)

Lessons for Today: A Desire for God

According to Peter, genuine believers "long for the pure spiritual milk" (1 Pet. 2:2). Having experienced the goodness of the Lord, we naturally desire more of him. As we seek this closer relationship with the Lord, he empowers us to break free from the destructive patterns of our former way of living—the malice, deceit, hypocrisy, envy, and slander that once gripped our hearts. These harmful behaviors are set aside as we intentionally seek the Lord, immerse ourselves in his word, and grow in our relationship with him. Righteous living flows from knowing God and loving him. Each of us should "long" for that meaningful and transformative relationship with him. As the Psalmist proclaims, "As a deer pants for flowing streams, so pants my soul for you, O God. My soul thirsts for God, for the living God. When shall I come and appear before God?" (Ps. 42:1–2)

Does this Psalm resonate with you? Do you feel that deep yearning in your heart to catch just a glimpse of his glory and to experience his presence in your life? Do you thirst for him? Far too often, people who profess to be believers treat God as little more than an accessory they have added to their lives rather than someone they desperately need. There is no meaningful relationship, no real priority placed on their faith. They say they believe in God, but their lives show little evidence of that belief. That is not the kind of relationship God wants.

If you find yourself feeling disconnected from God but desire a deeper, more meaningful relationship with him, you cannot expect it to simply happen on its own. Like any close relationship, cultivating a deep connection with God requires effort. Just as you might schedule intentional time with a spouse or close friend, set aside regular time to be with God. Make it a priority. A good place to start is by dedicating a certain amount of time every day to prayer, reading Scripture, or worship. If it matters to you, you will *make* time for it. If you struggle with discipline or forgetfulness, create a plan for accountability. Set reminders on your phone to pause and connect with God. Ask a spouse or trusted friend to check in with you and encourage you to remain consistent. You could also keep a journal to record your prayers and reflections on Scripture. These practical steps can help you build and deepen your relationship with the Lord.

As James reminds us, "Draw near to God, and he will draw near to you" (James 4:8). When you take a step toward him, he will meet you at that step. So, "long for the pure spiritual milk, that by it you may grow up into salvation."

Chapter 5

Live Honorably Among the Gentiles
(1 Peter 2:11–3:7)

11 Beloved, I urge you as sojourners and exiles to abstain from the passions of the flesh, which wage war against your soul. 12 Keep your conduct among the Gentiles honorable, so that when they speak against you as evildoers, they may see your good deeds and glorify God on the day of visitation. 13 Be subject for the Lord's sake to every human institution, whether it be to the emperor as supreme, 14 or to governors as sent by him to punish those who do evil and to praise those who do good. 15 For this is the will of God, that by doing good you should put to silence the ignorance of foolish people. 16 Live as people who are free, not using your freedom as a cover-up for evil, but living as servants of God. 17 Honor everyone. Love the brotherhood. Fear God. Honor the emperor.

18 Servants, be subject to your masters with all respect, not only to the good and gentle but also to the unjust. 19 For this is a gracious thing, when, mindful of God, one endures sorrows while suffering unjustly. 20 For what credit is it if, when you sin and are beaten for it, you endure? But if when you do good and suffer for it you endure, this is a gracious thing in the sight of God. 21 For to this you have been called, because Christ also suffered for you, leaving you an example, so that you might follow in his steps. 22 He committed no sin, neither was deceit found in his mouth. 23 When he was reviled, he did not revile in return; when he suffered, he did not threaten, but continued entrusting

Live Honorably Among the Gentiles (1 Peter 2:11–3:7)

himself to him who judges justly. **24** He himself bore our sins in his body on the tree, that we might die to sin and live to righteousness. By his wounds you have been healed. **25** For you were straying like sheep, but have now returned to the Shepherd and Overseer of your souls.

3:1 Likewise, wives, be subject to your own husbands, so that even if some do not obey the word, they may be won without a word by the conduct of their wives, **2** when they see your respectful and pure conduct. **3** Do not let your adorning be external—the braiding of hair and the putting on of gold jewelry, or the clothing you wear—**4** but let your adorning be the hidden person of the heart with the imperishable beauty of a gentle and quiet spirit, which in God's sight is very precious. **5** For this is how the holy women who hoped in God used to adorn themselves, by submitting to their own husbands, **6** as Sarah obeyed Abraham, calling him lord. And you are her children, if you do good and do not fear anything that is frightening. **7** Likewise, husbands, live with your wives in an understanding way, showing honor to the woman as the weaker vessel, since they are heirs with you of the grace of life, so that your prayers may not be hindered.

Having just reminded his readers that they are a royal priesthood, a holy nation, and full members of God's people through the Messiah, Peter now turns to how this identity ought to shape the way they live in the non-believing world. In this section of 1 Peter, we will explore how believers are called to live honorably among the Gentiles and show proper respect and submission within society, government, and the home.

Peter opens this section by urging his readers, whom he identifies as sojourners and resident aliens,[1] "to abstain from the passions of the flesh,

---

1   "Resident aliens" is Craig Keener's translation (*1 Peter: A Commentary* [Grand Rapids:

Live Honorably Among the Gentiles (1 Peter 2:11–3:7)

which wage war against your soul" (1 Pet. 2:11). As God's children with an everlasting inheritance kept in heaven (1 Pet. 1:4, 14, 17), believers are to recognize that this present world is not their permanent home. Therefore, they should not remain attached to the temporary things of this world. As a distinct and "holy" people (1 Pet. 1:14–16), they must resist those "passions of the flesh" that fight against their "soul" (ψυχή)—a term here that refers to the "seat and center of the inner human life," a person's essence "that transcends the earthly."[2] In Romans, Paul similarly speaks of an internal "war" between his mind's desire to obey God and his flesh's desire to sin (Rom. 7:15, 22–25). He notes that the flesh resists submitting to God's Torah (Rom. 8:7), but those who walk according to the Spirit are empowered to fulfill the Torah's righteous requirements (Rom. 8:4). In the same way, Peter's readers are being sanctified by the Spirit (1 Pet. 1:2), enabling them to win the war against the sinful desires of the flesh as they seek to walk in obedience and holiness.

Even though Peter's readers are members of God's people and distinct from the world, they still must live within the world (cf. John 17:15; 1 Cor. 5:10). Hence, Peter writes, "Keep your conduct among the Gentiles honorable" (1 Pet. 2:12). Here, when Peter uses the term "Gentiles," he is not referring to non-Jews since his own readers are mostly non-Jews. While "Gentiles" does often refer generally to non-Jews—including non-Jews who follow the Messiah—in the context of 1 Peter, it consistently refers to *unbelieving* Gentiles.[3] Paul, also writing to a primarily Gentile audience, occasionally uses the term in the same way: "you must

---

Baker Academic, 2021), xxxix). I disagree with the ESV's translation of "exiles" here. See my note on 1 Peter 1:1.

[2] BDAG, 979–980.

[3] See Duane F. Watson: "'Gentiles' does not refer to non-Jews as in postexilic Jewish tradition (Isa. 24–27; Ezek. 38–39; Zech. 9–14) but to all unbelievers. It is a natural extension of the close association of Israel and believers in the letter (2:9–10). The reference is to one's stance toward faith, not ethnicity" ("First Peter," in *First and Second Peter*, by Duane F. Watson and Terrance Callan, PCNT [Grand Rapids: Baker Academic, 2012], 58–59).

Live Honorably Among the Gentiles (1 Peter 2:11–3:7)

no longer walk as the Gentiles do…They are darkened in their understanding, alienated from the life of God" (Eph. 4:17–18).

Why ought believers live honorably among the Gentiles? Peter explains that it is "so that when they speak against you as evildoers, they may see your good deeds and glorify God on the day of visitation" (1 Pet. 2:12). The readers of 1 Peter no longer took part in the practices common among their Gentile neighbors (1 Pet. 4:3–4). These cultural practices included, for instance, "many events involving idolatry, such as business lunches in temples and local festivals honoring the gods."[4] Refusing to participate in these practices was viewed as "a hostile act against the gods that threatened family, neighbors, and city."[5] Because of this, Peter's readers were maligned "as evildoers." Thus, he encourages them to keep their conduct honorable, trusting that their "good deeds" will silence slander and prompt their critics to glorify God. Although this strategy does not guarantee that these critics will come to faith, this kind of witness can at times lead to such an outcome.[6] Still, as Craig Keener notes, "at the very least the effort will be vindicated, and God glorified, on the day of judgment."[7]

Peter goes on to instruct his readers, "Be subject for the Lord's sake to every human institution" (1 Pet. 2:13). As noted above, one of the complaints against followers of Yeshua was that their beliefs and way of life were a threat to the public order. Therefore, Peter's instructions that follow are aimed at helping believers combat against those complaints. Peter tells believers to submit to governing authorities (1 Pet. 2:13–14), servants to submit to their masters (1 Pet. 2:18–25), and wives to submit

---

4 Watson, "First Peter," 59.
5 Kelly D. Liebengood, *Reading 1 Peter After Supersessionism: Jewish Apostolic Affirmation of Gentile Israelhood* (Eugene, OR: Cascade, 2025), 64.
6 For instance, as Keener notes, Justin Martyr "was later converted through witnessing Christians' lack of fear in the face of death" (*1 Peter*, 162). Keener cites Justin Martyr, *2 Apol.* 12.
7 Keener, *1 Peter*, 162.

to their unbelieving husbands (1 Pet. 3:1–6). These instructions fall under what are known as "household codes"—cultural standards that outlined proper behavior within families and society.[8] In the ancient world, following these ethical norms was essential for being viewed as respectable members of the community. While believers are called to be holy and faithful to their biblical convictions, they are also to show respect for human institutions and cultural norms in order to avoid harming their witness. Peter adopts these common ethical codes (while making slight modifications) so that the honorable behavior of his readers might silence their critics and shame those who speak against them (1 Pet. 2:15; 3:16).

One way that believers demonstrate honorable conduct among the Gentiles is by submitting to "every human institution," which includes various civil authorities such as "the emperor as supreme, or to governors as sent by him to punish those who do evil and to praise those who do good" (1 Pet. 2:13–14). Applied to a modern American context, the "supreme" authority might refer to the federal government, while "governors" could represent local officials, such as lawmakers and police officers. Following Peter's instruction, believers are called to be responsible citizens and show respect for these authorities to the best of their ability. They submit to authority "for the Lord's sake" (1 Pet. 2:13)—in other words, to be faithful witnesses on the Lord's behalf. Peter writes, "For this is the will of God" (1 Pet. 2:15), indicating that this is the kind of conduct God desires from his people as they live in society. Importantly, submitting "for the Lord's sake" also reminds believers that while they should strive to respect human authority, their ultimate loyalty is to God, and his commands always take precedence. As Paul J. Achtemeier explains, the phrase "for the Lord's sake" qualifies submission to human

---

8   For an in-depth explanation of the function of household codes, see Craig S. Keener, "Family and Household" in *Dictionary of New Testament Background*, ed. Craig A. Evans and Stanley E. Porter (Downers Grove, IL: IVP Academic, 2000), 353-368.

Live Honorably Among the Gentiles (1 Peter 2:11–3:7)

institutions "by placing it within the larger context of obedience to God; one is not to be subordinate in matters that go counter to God's will."[9]

Peter writes that "by doing good" his readers "should put to silence the ignorance of foolish people" (1 Pet. 2:15). Rather than defying human institutions, Peter says that believers should conduct themselves "honorably" as a means of quieting the accusations against them. The hope is that governors would cease punishing them and instead "praise those who do good" (1 Pet. 2:14). However, once again, this is no guarantee. As Keener writes, "Although it is God's will…for them to silence accusers by good deeds (2:15), Peter explicitly allows that God might will them to suffer for doing good (3:17; 4:19)."[10] Believers should seek to avoid conflict with the world, but Peter recognizes that this is not always possible. In many ways, biblical morality aligns with the broader society's understanding of what is "good," so living according to God's ways often goes hand-in-hand with being a good citizen.[11] However, there are also clear areas where godly values differ significantly from those of the culture. In such cases, believers must be willing to suffer for doing what is right (1 Pet. 3:14, 17; 4:3–4).

As resident aliens in this world, believers must constantly navigate the tension between honoring God and living peacefully within a society that often opposes his ways. Sometimes, being faithful to God means standing against cultural norms and enduring hardship or persecution as a result. An example of this from the Hebrew Scriptures is found in Exodus 1:15–17, where the king of Egypt commanded the Hebrew midwives to kill all male Hebrew infants. Obeying that order would have violated God's commands, but resisting it violated the command of the king. The midwives chose to obey God above all else, refusing to submit to an unjust decree. Wisdom is learning how to discern when to submit and when to resist. Believers should strive, as far as it depends on them,

---

9   Paul J. Achtemeir, *1 Peter*, Hermeneia (Minneapolis: Fortress Press, 1996), 182.
10 Keener, *1 Peter*, 171.
11 Watson, "First Peter," 65.

Live Honorably Among the Gentiles (1 Peter 2:11–3:7)

to "live peaceably with all" (Rom. 12:18). Yet they must also be prepared to courageously stand for what is right, even when it means facing persecution from the culture or government.

Peter continues by saying, "Live as people who are free, not using your freedom as a cover-up for evil, but living as servants of God" (1 Pet. 2:16). In the Messiah, believers have been set free from the ultimate control of earthly authorities, because their true citizenship belongs to a higher, eternal kingdom. Their identity, purpose, and destiny are not defined by human rulers. They should recognize and rejoice in their freedom. However, this freedom must not be used as an excuse to act dishonorably or to rebel unnecessarily against civil authority. To misuse that freedom in such a way would be to turn it into a "cover-up for evil" (cf. Gal. 5:13). Instead, believers are called to submit to human authorities as an expression of their service to God, who is their true authority. As God's servants, they are expected to show honor to everyone, love fellow believers, fear God, and even honor those in positions of civil leadership (1 Pet. 2:17). As Peter writes, "For this is the will of God" (1 Pet. 2:15). Yet, while believers are to show proper respect to human authorities, once again, their highest allegiance remains with God.

The next part of Peter's household code addresses how servants are to relate to their masters. Peter writes, "Servants, be subject to your masters with all respect, not only to the good and gentle but also to the unjust" (1 Pet. 2:18). The relationship between servants and masters is another form of submission to human authority (1 Pet. 2:13). Peter instructs servants to submit to their masters with all respect, whether those masters are kind or harsh. Even if they suffer mistreatment or abuse under unjust authority, Peter reassures them that enduring such suffering for doing good is "a gracious thing in the sight of God" (1 Pet. 2:19–20). He then points to Yeshua as the ultimate example of righteous conduct in the face of undeserved suffering (1 Pet. 2:21–25).

Modern readers often find the Bible's instructions about master-slave relationships troubling. It is important to understand that Peter is not endorsing the "human institution" (1 Pet. 2:13) of slavery by commenting on it. Slavery was part of the social structure of his time, and believers had to navigate this less-than-ideal reality as best they could. Peter's guidance to slaves reflects a pragmatic concern: helping believers live in a way that brings glory to God and serves as a powerful witness in a society where slavery was deeply entrenched. His focus is on encouraging faithful conduct within the reality they faced, not on validating the system itself.[12] It is also important to note that Scripture does not call for institutions like slavery to be reinstalled in modern times. While the underlying *principles* of Peter's teaching (such as honoring God through humble and respectful conduct) are timeless, the specific *cultural context* in which those principles were previously applied is not meant to be carried forward to today. Keener puts this point well:

> The eschatological people of God must still function within society, morally distinct but socially honorable. The instructions regarding subjects of kings (2:13), slaves (2:18–25), and wives of nonbelievers (3:1–6) do not mandate maintaining monarchy, slavery, or patriarchal forms of marriage in all societies. (Indeed, attempts to resurrect those structures against current social paradigms would undercut the attempts at peace with society for which these instructions were designed.) These are human institutions (2:13), and Peter himself recognizes that they may act unjustly (2:19). They do illustrate the principle of honoring social roles where possible for the sake of Christian witness (2:12–13).[13]

---

12 See Keener, *1 Peter*, 167: "Peter addresses slaves in their circumstances; he does not endorse (or condemn) the institution of slavery itself. Addressing the institution would not have been of practical, pastoral relevance to members of his audience…For that matter, abolition was barely even an option in first-century discussions of hypothetical social ethics."

13 Keener, *1 Peter*, 146.

Live Honorably Among the Gentiles (1 Peter 2:11–3:7)

Peter concludes his instructions to servants by urging his readers to follow the example of Yeshua: "For to this you have been called, because Christ also suffered for you, leaving you an example, so that you might follow in his steps" (1 Pet. 2:21). Just as Yeshua endured unjust suffering without retaliating (1 Pet. 2:22), so too should his followers respond to mistreatment with trust in God, "who judges justly" (1 Pet. 2:23). Yeshua's response to injustice was to entrust himself to the Father, and believers are called to do the same, knowing that ultimate vindication will come. Just as Yeshua was raised from the dead, so too will they be vindicated in the world to come.

Chapter 2 of 1 Peter concludes with Peter affirming Yeshua as the Shepherd and Overseer of their souls. Through his sacrifice on the tree, he has brought redemption and healing. As Shepherd and Overseer, he continues to guide, protect, and teach his people in the way of righteousness (1 Pet. 2:24–25).

The next section of Peter's household code focuses on the relationship between husbands and wives. He instructs wives to "be subject to your own husbands," even in cases where their husbands "do not obey the word"—in other words, even if they are not believers (1 Pet. 1:1).[14] Once again, there is an apologetic purpose behind this instruction. The aim is that the husband "may be won without a word" by observing his wife's "respectful and pure conduct" (1 Pet. 1:1–2). This offers another clear example of the tension believers face between loyalty to the Messiah and maintaining honorable conduct within a non-believing society—a tension that can even arise within one's own family! In the Greco-Roman world, wives were expected not only to submit to their husbands but also to follow their husbands' religion.[15] Obviously, a wife who put her

---

14 See Achtemeier, *1 Peter*, 209: "While the phrase καὶ εἴ τινες ("even if some") implies that not all husbands of Christian wives are nonbelievers, it is clear that the verse is directed to those Christian wives for whom that is in fact the case: the interrogative particle εἴ states a fact here, not a hypothetical possibility."

15 See Scot McKnight: "Asia Minor permitted freedoms to women, including some kind of

faith in the Messiah could not comply with that cultural expectation, so she had to navigate the delicate balance of preserving peace at home while hoping her respectful and pure conduct might lead her husband to embrace *her* religion instead.[16]

Peter continues by saying, "Do not let your adorning be external," and he mentions examples such as elaborate hairstyles, jewelry, and fine clothing (1 Pet. 3:3). This is not a blanket ban on wearing nice clothing or jewelry, but a warning against excess, which was considered immodest "and could lead to the woman and her husband being dishonored for such extravagance."[17] If a wife hopes to "win" her husband, she must continue to show him honor and respect. Instead of excessively focusing on outward appearance, wives are called to adorn themselves with "the hidden person of the heart with the imperishable beauty of a gentle and quiet spirit" (1 Pet. 3:4). Unlike external beauty, which fades over time, "the hidden person of the heart" that exhibits the virtues of "a gentle and quiet spirit" possesses an "imperishable beauty" that endures forever.

Peter points to the "holy women" as the examples for these wives to follow (1 Pet. 3:5). Since he specifically cites Sarah in this context (1 Pet. 3:6), the "holy women" he is likely alluding to are the matriarchs of Israel—Sarah, Rebecca, Rachel, and Leah—who placed their hope in God, submitted to their husbands, and embodied humility, gentleness, and respect.[18] Peter urges believing wives to adopt the same posture of trust in God as they seek to influence their husbands through respectful and pure conduct. He concludes his instructions to wives by affirming their identity as daughters of Sarah—part of the family of Israel through

---

religious freedom; however, most scholars are agreed that when a woman struck out on her own and joined a religion different from her husband's, that could be seen as an act of insubordination" (*1 Peter*, NIVAC [Grand Rapids: Zondervan, 1996], 184).

16   Achtemier, *1 Peter*, 211.
17   Watson, "First Peter," 74.
18   See Watson, "First Peter," 75: "The article before 'holy wives' indicates a specific group, probably the wives of Israel's patriarchs, as the following example of Sarah indicates. These wives include Sarah (Abraham), Rebecca (Isaac), and Leah and Rachel (Jacob)."

the Messiah—saying, "And you are her children, if you do good and do not fear anything that is frightening" (1 Pet. 3:6). These women are encouraged not to be ruled by fear, but to place their confidence in God, their highest authority.

Peter now turns to give a brief exhortation to husbands. In contrast to his instructions for wives, Peter assumes that these husbands are married to fellow believers.[19] This assumption fits with the cultural norm of the time: wives were generally expected to adopt their husband's religion, so a believing husband married to an unbelieving wife would have been uncommon.[20] Peter instructs husbands to "live with your wives in an understanding way, showing honor to the woman as the weaker vessel" (1 Pet. 3:7). In the ancient Greco-Roman world, women were often regarded as inferior to men in areas such as intellect, morality, physical strength, and spirituality.[21] However, Peter does not share the cultural views that women by nature are morally, intellectually, or spiritually inferior. His earlier instructions in verses 1–2 make that clear. Instead, he likely has in mind that women are generally physically weaker than men and have a lower social standing in the culture.[22] In keeping with biblical values that call for special care toward those in weaker or more vulnerable positions, Peter urges husbands to treat their wives with sensitivity and understanding. Furthermore, although women were often regarded as inferior in the wider culture, Peter tells husbands to show their wives "honor" and view them as co-heirs of the grace of life (1 Pet. 3:7). This reflects a deliberate departure from prevailing societal attitudes toward women. As Achtemeier writes:

---

19 Keener, *1 Peter*, 242.
20 Watson, "First Peter," 76.
21 Watson, "First Peter," 76. Watson cites Plato, *Leg.* 6.781A; *Resp.* 5.455D– 456A; *Let. Aris.* 250–51; Philo, *Ebr.* 55; Tacitus, *Ann.* 3.34
22 Keener, *1 Peter*, 245.

Live Honorably Among the Gentiles (1 Peter 2:11–3:7)

> The description of the women as coheirs of the grace of life forms a grammatical parallel to their description as weaker vessels and gives further reason for men not to adopt the normal cultural attitude toward them, since in God's eyes, as heirs of grace, men and women stand on the same level.[23]

Peter concludes his instructions to husbands by emphasizing that a husband's treatment of his wife is so crucial that his prayers can be hindered if he fails to honor her (1 Pet. 3:7). God listens to the prayers of the righteous but resists those who do wrong (1 Pet. 3:12; cf. Ps. 34:15–16). Instead of embracing the cultural view of women as inferior, husbands are called to recognize their wives as equal heirs in the faith and treat them accordingly.

Lessons for Today: Seek the Welfare of the City

The consistent message of 1 Peter is that our hope rests in the assurance of future salvation (1 Pet. 1:4, 8–12; 5:10). We don't need to be anxious about all that is wrong in the present world. The Messiah will return and set all things right in his timing. Our responsibility is to remain faithful and conduct ourselves honorably, no matter our current situation.

But is Peter suggesting that believers should just be content with the world as it is? Do we have any responsibility in improving it right now? Peter does say that our good deeds and honorable conduct may lead others to glorify God (1 Pet. 2:12; 3:1–2), and the natural outcome of more people becoming followers of the Messiah is a better world. Historically, the spread of Christian beliefs and values has played a significant role in advancing human health and prosperity, abolishing slavery, and

---

23 Achtemeier, *1 Peter*, 218.

promoting education in many societies.[24] While our ultimate hope rests in the world to come, the good deeds of believers can still bring real change here and now.

Peter's instructions to his readers remind me of the instructions the prophet Jeremiah gave to the Jewish exiles in Babylon. Jeremiah encouraged them to make the most of their difficult circumstances, urging them to settle down, plant gardens, get married and have children, and even pray for and seek the welfare of the city where they had been scattered (Jer. 29:4–7). In other words, live your life, do good deeds, and make a positive difference wherever you can in your own city because "in its welfare you will find your welfare" (Jer. 29:7).

What does it look like to "seek the welfare of the city" today? It means actively investing in the places where we live. If we have opportunities to influence leaders or shape public policy, we should take them. That might mean voting or advocating for causes that reflect biblical values in our own society. Sadly, too many believers want to tell the world to go to hell and just withdraw from society altogether until the Messiah returns.

---

[24] Christian missionaries have long contributed to expanding access to education and healthcare by establishing schools and hospitals in areas with limited resources. Numerous studies show how their work not only fostered learning but also paved the way for progress in science, medicine, and technology, leading to significant improvements in quality of life in Africa, the Americas, Australia, and Asia. See, e.g., Federico Mantovanelli, *The Protestant Legacy: Missions and Literacy in India* (paper presented at the Economic Theory Seminar, Department of Economics, University of California, Riverside, February 4, 2014); Tomila V. Lankina and Lullit Getachew, "Competitive Religious Entrepreneurs: Christian Missionaries and Female Education in Colonial and Post-Colonial India," *BJPS* 43, no. 1 (2013), 103–131; Francisco A. Gallego and Robert Woodberry, "Christian Missionaries and Education in Former African Colonies: How Competition Mattered, *JAE* 19, no. 3 (2010), 294–329; Rossella Calvi and Federico Mantovanelli, "Long-Term effects of access to health care: Medical missions in colonial India," *JDE* 135 (2018), 285–303; Yuyu Chen, Hui Wang, and Se Yan, "The Long-Term Effects of Protestant Activities in China," *SSRN* (2014), 1–57; Ying Bai and James Kai-sing Kung, "Diffusing Knowledge While Spreading God's Message: Protestantism and Economic Prosperity in China, 1840–1920," *JEEA* 13, no. 4 (2015), 669–698.

Live Honorably Among the Gentiles (1 Peter 2:11–3:7)

But I don't think that attitude is biblical. Neither Jeremiah nor Peter advocated for withdrawing from society entirely. They both assumed that believers would be interacting with society and that they could have a positive impact for God's glory and for the welfare of others.

I am reminded of the 18th-century evangelical Christians in England who played a key role in ending the transatlantic slave trade. Led by William Wilberforce, these believers organized petitions, gave public lectures, and published literature to stir public opposition to slavery. Their persistence eventually built enough momentum to pressure the government into passing laws to abolish the trade.[25] In much the same way today, God continues to work through faithful followers of Messiah to promote justice and righteousness in the world. Believers still champion causes such as the fight against abortion and sex trafficking—and by God's grace, they often make a real difference. It is clear that the world has been profoundly shaped for the better by committed Christians living out their faith.

At the same time, as followers of Yeshua, we do not entertain utopian fantasies. Though we may work toward meaningful improvements over time, we understand that our present world will never be perfect. The world remains broken because of sin, and no political leader or legislation can turn "Babylon" into the New Jerusalem. Injustice, corruption, and suffering will persist as long as sin exists. While we strive to influence our communities for God's glory, we recognize that this world is not our true home. Only when Yeshua returns to establish his kingdom will everything be made right. Until then, we do our best to live honorably among those around us, looking forward to the day when his perfect reign begins.

---

25 Bruce L. Shelley, *Church History in Plain Language*, 4th ed. (Grand Rapids: Zondervan, 2013), 384–386.

Chapter 6

Suffer for Righteousness' Sake
(1 Peter 3:8–22)

8 Finally, all of you, have unity of mind, sympathy, brotherly love, a tender heart, and a humble mind. **9** Do not repay evil for evil or reviling for reviling, but on the contrary, bless, for to this you were called, that you may obtain a blessing. **10** For "Whoever desires to love life and see good days, let him keep his tongue from evil and his lips from speaking deceit; **11** let him turn away from evil and do good; let him seek peace and pursue it. **12** For the eyes of the Lord are on the righteous, and his ears are open to their prayer. But the face of the Lord is against those who do evil."

13 Now who is there to harm you if you are zealous for what is good? **14** But even if you should suffer for righteousness' sake, you will be blessed. Have no fear of them, nor be troubled, **15** but in your hearts honor Christ the Lord as holy, always being prepared to make a defense to anyone who asks you for a reason for the hope that is in you; yet do it with gentleness and respect, **16** having a good conscience, so that, when you are slandered, those who revile your good behavior in Christ may be put to shame. **17** For it is better to suffer for doing good, if that should be God's will, than for doing evil.

18 For Christ also suffered once for sins, the righteous for the unrighteous, that he might bring us to God, being put to death in the flesh but made alive in the spirit, **19** in which he went

Suffer for Righteousness' Sake (1 Peter 3:8–22)

> and proclaimed to the spirits in prison, **20** because they formerly did not obey, when God's patience waited in the days of Noah, while the ark was being prepared, in which a few, that is, eight persons, were brought safely through water. **21** Baptism, which corresponds to this, now saves you, not as a removal of dirt from the body but as an appeal to God for a good conscience, through the resurrection of Jesus Christ, **22** who has gone into heaven and is at the right hand of God, with angels, authorities, and powers having been subjected to him.

Peter had just given instructions on how believers should live honorably among unbelievers, carefully navigating the tension between obedience to God and respectful submission to human authorities. The hope is that through their good deeds and honorable behavior, believers might quiet their critics and even lead some unbelievers to glorify God (1 Pet. 2:12). However, Peter now goes on to acknowledge that doing good may still result in suffering and that such suffering may, in fact, be God's will (1 Pet. 3:17).

Peter urges his readers to cultivate "unity of mind" and "sympathy" among themselves.[1] This does not require complete agreement on every issue, but rather a spirit of mutual respect and an attentiveness to one another's needs, recognizing their shared goal to glorify God. He calls them to exhibit "brotherly love" and "a tender heart," reflecting a deep commitment and sincere compassion for one another. Lastly, he instructs

---

1   There is a question about whether 1 Peter 3:8 addresses how believers should relate to fellow believers or to unbelievers. I understand this verse as Peter instructing his readers on how to treat one another within the community of faith, especially since traits like "brotherly love" are more naturally understood as referring to relationships among fellow believers. However, for a different interpretation, see Scot McKnight, *1 Peter*, NIVAC (Grand Rapids: Zondervan, 1996), 200.

Suffer for Righteousness' Sake (1 Peter 3:8–22)

them to have "a humble mind," which involves a servant-like attitude that puts the needs of others before one's own needs (1 Pet. 1:8).[2]

After encouraging believers to exhibit brotherly love, unity, and humility within the faith community, Peter shifts his focus to how they should respond when faced with mistreatment from those outside the faith: "Do not repay evil for evil or reviling for reviling, but on the contrary, bless, for to this you were called, that you may obtain a blessing" (1 Pet. 3:9). This instruction echoes Yeshua's teaching on nonretaliation in Matthew 5:38–48. Instead of responding to insults with violence, Peter tells believers to actively "bless" those who mistreat them. Even if blessing does not change the offender, this response is the path to receiving blessing from God. To support this, Peter quotes Psalm 34:12–16, which promises that God favors those who guard their speech, pursue peace, and turn away from evil (1 Pet. 3:10¬–11). The psalm also warns that "the eyes of the Lord are on the righteous" and that "the face of the Lord is against those who do evil" (1 Pet. 3:12). In other words, no one can escape God's attention. He is always watching, so believers must make sure that they are on God's side and always doing good.

One benefit of responding to evil with blessing is that people are generally less inclined to want to harm those who are "zealous for what is good" (1 Pet 3:13).[3] Still, Peter recognizes that even those who are righteous may suffer persecution. When that happens, believers have no reason to "fear." Their suffering is "for righteousness' sake" (1 Pet. 3:14), and as Yeshua taught in the Sermon on the Mount (Matt. 5:10), they are truly blessed. Because their blessing is secure, believers need not be intimidated by those who oppose them (cf. Heb. 13:6). Their confidence rests in a salvation to come—a lasting inheritance awaiting them at the end of the age (1 Pet. 1:3–12).

---

2 Paul J. Achtemeier, *1 Peter*, Hermeneia (Minneapolis: Fortress Press, 1996), 223. See also Duane F. Watson, "First Peter," in *First and Second Peter*, by Duane F. Watson and Terrance Callan, PCNT (Grand Rapids: Baker Academic, 2012), 58–59.

3 Craig Keener, *1 Peter: A Commentary* (Grand Rapids: Baker Academic, 2021), 257.

Suffer for Righteousness' Sake (1 Peter 3:8–22)

Peter's exhortation not to be afraid is rooted in Isaiah 8:12–13 and flows directly into his next instruction: "but in your hearts honor Christ the Lord as holy" (1 Pet. 3:15). In the Isaiah passage, God tells his people, "Do not call conspiracy all that this people calls conspiracy, and do not fear what they fear, nor be in dread. But the LORD of hosts, him you shall honor as holy." Peter had already drawn from Isaiah 8:14 in the previous chapter (1 Pet. 2:8), identifying the Messiah as the "stumbling stone." Now, he draws from the surrounding verses to make a similar point: those facing persecution should revere the true "rock"—Messiah the Lord—instead of fearing their persecutors. Surprisingly, Peter applies this passage from Isaiah to the Messiah, even though in its original context Isaiah was speaking about the LORD (YHWH).[4] While persecutors may cause suffering, their power is temporary and limited to this world. But the hope believers possess lies in God's promise of salvation and an everlasting inheritance beyond this world. Therefore, Peter urges believers to honor the Messiah as holy, affirming their full allegiance to him above all else.

Peter instructs his readers to always be prepared "to make a defense to anyone who asks you for a reason for the hope that is in you" (1 Pet. 3:15). The word translated "make a defense" is ἀπολογία in Greek (from which we get the English term "apologetics"), and it refers to making a reasonable argument.[5] According to Peter, every believer should always

---

4   Keener, *1 Peter*, 260. Paul similarly applies passages from the Hebrew Scriptures that originally referred to YHWH to the Messiah (e.g., Rom 10:9–13; Phil. 2:11). For an in-depth examination of how YHWH texts are applied to the Messiah in the apostolic writings, see Robert M. Bowman Jr. and J. Ed Komoszewski, *The Incarnate Christ and His Critics: A Biblical Defense* (Grand Rapids: Kregel Academic, 2024), especially chapters 25 and 26. See also Scott Brazil, *Jesus and YHWH-Texts in the Synoptic Gospels* (New York: T&T Clark, 2024); David B. Capes, *Old Testament Yahweh Texts in Paul's Christology*, Library of Early Christology (Waco, TX: Baylor University Press, 2017); David B. Capes, *The Divine Christ: Paul, the Lord Jesus, and the Scriptures of Israel*, Acadia Studies in Bible and Theology (Grand Rapids: Baker Academic, 2018).

5   BDAG, 102.

Suffer for Righteousness' Sake (1 Peter 3:8–22)

be prepared to offer a thoughtful and reasoned argument in support of their "hope." In the context of 1 Peter, this "hope" refers to the confident expectation of salvation and future inheritance through the Messiah (cf. 1 Peter 1:3, 20–21).[6] Instead of fearing those who are hostile toward them (1 Pet. 3:14), believers are called to be equipped to confidently explain why they have hope in the Messiah and answer their questions and criticisms.

The reasoned arguments of believers must be offered "with gentleness and respect" (1 Pet. 3:15). Rather than responding to critics with aggression or hostility, believers are to engage others respectfully, aiming to persuade them through calm and gracious dialogue. This "good behavior" puts to shame those who slander believers. Furthermore, Peter acknowledges that suffering may, at times, be "God's will." And if it is God's will that one should suffer, it would be "better to suffer for doing good" (1 Pet. 3:17). As Duane Watson writes, "Suffering for doing good is a test from God (1:6–7; 4:12–16, 19). Christ exemplified this suffering (2:21–24; 3:18; 4:1), and God approves and rewards such a righteous sufferer, as he approved Christ."[7] Furthermore, when believers remain faithful and continue to do what is right despite opposition or mistreatment, their endurance becomes a powerful testimony. It shows the watching world that the gospel is worth suffering for, which is something no one would willingly endure for a lie. This lived-out witness is itself a type of "apologetics."

Having just affirmed that it is better to suffer for doing good, Peter now turns to the ultimate example of this truth: the suffering of the Messiah himself (cf. 1 Pet. 2:21–25). Peter writes, "for Christ also suffered" (1 Pet. 3:18). However, Yeshua's suffering was far more than an example. His suffering and death were "for sins," indicating that his death was a sacrificial act of redemption.[8] Just as Levitical animal sacrifices allowed

---

6   Keener, *1 Peter*, 260.
7   Watson, "First Peter," 86.
8   See Watson, "First Peter," 87–88: "His was clearly a sacrificial death (1:19; 2:24) since the

worshipers to draw near to God at the tabernacle or temple, Yeshua's death functioned to "bring us to God." But unlike the repeated animal sacrifices, his sacrifice was made "once" (cf. Heb. 7:27; 9:12, 26–28). Though completely "righteous," he died on behalf of the "unrighteous" in order to reconcile them to God. Here, Peter clearly affirms vicarious suffering—the righteous Messiah suffering in the place of the unrighteous, bearing the penalty for sin so that they might be restored to God.[9] His words may echo the imagery of Isaiah 53, the well-known passage about the suffering servant, which Peter quoted earlier (1 Pet. 2:24–25). In Isaiah, the servant—a figure whom the New Testament identifies as Yeshua (cf. Luke 22:37; Acts 8:32–25)—takes upon himself the punishment that the people deserved for their transgressions. Though innocent and righteous, the servant suffers on behalf of the guilty, making it possible for them to receive forgiveness, healing, and reconciliation with God.

Peter continues by stating that Yeshua was "put to death in the flesh but made alive in the spirit" (1 Pet. 3:18). This and the following verse have sparked much debate.[10] For example, some have taken "made alive in the spirit" to mean that after Yeshua's physical death on the cross, his spirit remained conscious and active prior to his bodily resurrection. According to this view, during that interim period, Yeshua's spirit descended into Hades—the abode of the dead—and proclaimed the gospel to the disembodied spirits residing there, "the spirits in prison" (1 Pet. 3:19).[11] However, the phrase "put to death in the flesh" could also be rendered "put to death *by* the flesh"—that is, by humans. Similarly,

---

phrase 'for sins' (*peri hamartion*) is used in the LXX (Lev. 5:6–7; 6:23; Ezek. 43:21) and the NT (Rom. 8:3; Heb. 5:3; 10:26; 1 John 2:2; 4:10) in connection with a sin offering."

9   See Keener, *1 Peter*, 268: "Christ's suffering as the righteous for the unrighteous fits the notion of vicarious suffering widely understood in antiquity."

10 Scot McKnight (*1 Peter*, 215) notes that there are three main interpretations among scholars: "(1) the descent-into-hell view, (2) the preexistent Christ view, and (3) the triumphal proclamation over the spirit-world view."

11 McKnight cites Leonhard Goppelt (*A Commentary on 1 Peter* [Grand Rapids: Eerdmans, 1993], 255-263) as one scholar who defends this view.

"made alive in the spirit" could be rendered "made alive *by* the Spirit," referring to the Holy Spirit's role in Yeshua's resurrection. According to this reading, Peter is saying that Yeshua was executed by humans ("flesh," cf. 1 Pet. 1:24) but raised to life by the Holy Spirit.[12] This interpretation fits the wider New Testament teaching (cf. Rom. 8:11; 1 Cor. 15:44–45) and is a more natural reading than the idea that Yeshua was "made alive" in the form of a conscious disembodied spirit prior to his bodily resurrection.

What does Peter mean when he says that Yeshua "went and proclaimed to the spirits in prison" (1 Pet. 3:19)? Who exactly are these "spirits in prison"? As noted above, one common interpretation suggests that Yeshua, in spirit form, descended into Hades to proclaim the gospel to the conscious human spirits dwelling there. According to this view, the "spirits in prison" are the souls of deceased humans who had died during Noah's flood (1 Pet. 3:20). Some proponents of this interpretation believe Yeshua's proclamation offered these individuals a postmortem "second chance" for salvation and release from their prison in Hades. However, several points make this interpretation unlikely. First, as Watson points out, the term πνεῦμα ("spirit") "is rarely used of a human, dead or alive, and if it is, it is qualified (cf. Heb. 12:23)."[13] Second, Scripture never uses the term φυλακή ("prison") to refer to the abode of the human dead.[14] As William J. Dalton writes, "Those commentators who advocate

---

12   See Achtemeier, *1 Peter*, 250: "A most natural construal of ζωοποιηθεὶς δὲ πνεύματι would be to take it as a dative of instrument: Christ was raised 'by the (divine) Spirit,' that is, by God, a central affirmation of the New Testament…It is hard to see how Christ could die 'by means of the flesh' so long as 'flesh' is understood either as Christ's own flesh or as a description of his human life. Yet the passive form of θανατωθεὶς indicates something done to Christ by others, and if one understands σάρξ to stand here for humanity as it does in 1:24, then it names the agency of Christ's death. In that case, it means that Christ was put to death by humans but raised by (God's) Spirit." However, note Watson's critique of this grammatical point ("First Peter," 89).

13   Watson, "First Peter," 89.

14   See William J. Dalton: "Nowhere in biblical literature is the world of the dead called

the 'last minute conversion' of Noah's wicked contemporaries…have to understand φυλακή in a somewhat forced fashion."[15] Third, if Yeshua's proclamation was meant to offer a second chance of salvation, it seems strange that such an offer would be limited to only those who died in Noah's generation. Why not extend the offer to others as well? Fourth, the very notion that people are given a second chance to receive salvation after death contradicts the broader teaching of Scripture. Hebrews 9:27 clearly states, "it is appointed for man to die once, and after that comes judgment" (cf. 2 Cor. 5:10).

Another proposed interpretation of this passage is that Yeshua's proclamation "in the spirit" did not occur between his death and resurrection, but instead took place *during the days of Noah*. As Guy Waters explains:

> The one who does the proclaiming of verse 19 is not the risen Jesus. It's Jesus who preaches, to be sure, but he preaches in the Holy Spirit. The timing of this proclamation is not the window between the death and ascension of Jesus Christ. It's during the lifetime of Noah. What, then, is Peter saying? He's saying that Noah, in the course of building the ark, bore testimony to the coming judgment of God. He was the "herald of righteousness," as Peter says in his second letter (2 Pet. 2:5). Noah preached in the power of the Holy Spirit, the Spirit whom Peter has earlier called "the Spirit of Christ" (1 Pet. 1:10).[16]

In other words, the Messiah, by the Holy Spirit, proclaimed the message of salvation through Noah to the people living in Noah's time, urging them to repent before the impending judgment. But due to their

---

φυλακή" (*Christ's Proclamation to the Spirits: A Study of 1 Peter 3:18–4:6* [Rome: Pontifical Biblical Institute, 1965], 158–159). See also Watson, "First Peter," 89–90.
15 Dalton, *Christ's Proclamation*, 158.
16 Guy Waters, "Does 1 Peter 3:19 Teach That Jesus Preached in Hell?" *The Gospel Coalition*, Oct. 21, 2019, www.thegospelcoalition.org.

disobedience and refusal to heed the message, God's patience ran out, and they perished in the flood. Their spirits now reside in "prison" (hell) because they "formerly did not obey" when the Messiah preached to them through Noah.[17] This interpretation fits well within the flow of Peter's overall message. Just before this, Peter urged his readers to always be ready to give a defense for their hope in the face of slander and suffering (1 Pet. 3:15–16), and this passage would continue that theme. Like Noah, believers must live in a world that is wicked and rejects God and his ways. Moreover, like Noah, believers are empowered by the Spirit of the Messiah to bear witness to their hope. And just as Noah and his family were delivered through judgment, so too will believers be rescued when the Messiah returns and judges the disobedient. Earlier, Peter wrote that the "Spirit of Christ" was at work in the Hebrew prophets (1 Peter 1:11–12), so it is not a stretch to think that this same "Spirit of Christ" spoke through Noah. However, while this interpretation is attractive, like the previous proposal, it also faces challenges. First, understanding πνεῦμα ("spirits") as human souls seems unnatural. Second, the Messiah's act of proclaiming in verse 19 appears to occur after the timeframe described in verse 20 ("because they formerly did not obey, when…"). As Keener writes, "Christ's preaching comes sometime after the flood rather than before it."[18]

A final interpretation suggests that the "spirits" to whom Yeshua preached are the "sons of God" from Genesis 6, and I find this to be the most likely reading.[19] Jewish tradition understands these sons of God as fallen angels who took human wives against God's will and were subsequently confined to a spiritual prison. According to this view, Yeshua's proclamation did not occur between his death and resurrection, nor

---

17 See Waters, "1 Peter 3:19": "That is, their souls, upon their deaths, were justly committed to hell to be punished for their sins."
18 Keener, *1 Peter*, 272.
19 According to Keener (*1 Peter*, 272), this is the interpretation held by "a majority of modern exegetes."

during the days of Noah, but instead during his ascension to heaven.[20] As he ascended, the Holy Spirit brought him to the place where these spirits were imprisoned, and there he proclaimed his victory over them. This interpretation has several strengths. For instance, Peter identifies these spirits as those who were disobedient "in the days of Noah." This fits with the Genesis 6 account of the "sons of God," which is situated within the broader Noah narrative. Moreover, Second Temple Jewish tradition, some of which is preserved in the book of 1 Enoch, explicitly links the "sons of God" in Genesis 6 to the fallen angels who are now imprisoned for marrying human women and producing the Nephilim (1 Enoch 10:4–6, 12–14; 21:7–10; Jubilees 5:6), and this idea of rebellious angels being confined also appears in 2 Peter 2:4 and Jude 6.[21] Remarkably, in 1 Enoch, as Enoch ascends to heaven, he "goes to these angels on his way, and announces their destruction."[22] This tradition closely parallels the account in 1 Peter 3:19, except that in Peter's passage it is the Messiah Yeshua who proclaims condemnation to the imprisoned spirits. Finally, this interpretation offers a more natural reading of the terms πνεῦμα ("spirits")[23] and φυλακή ("prison")[24] that aligns well with their usage in

---

20 Another possible interpretation combines elements of the first and third views. In this reading, Peter is describing Yeshua's conscious existence in the unseen realm between his death and resurrection, during which he interacts with the rebellious spirits from Genesis 6. See Michael S. Heiser, *The Unseen Realm: Recovering the Supernatural Worldview of the Bible* (Bellingham, WA: Lexham Press, 2015), 335–339.

21 Watson, "First Peter," 90.

22 Watson, "First Peter," 90. Watson cites 1 Enoch 12:4–6; 13.1–14.7; 15:1–16:3.

23 Keener (*1 Peter*, 273) cites several passages in biblical and extrabiblical Jewish and Christian literature that identify angels as spirits: 1 Enoch 15:4, 6–8, 10; 16:1; 19:1; 1QM 10.12; 12.8–9; 1QHa 5.25; 9.13; Heb. 1:7, 14; 1 Clement 36:3.

24 See Watson, "First Peter," 90: "Prison (*phylakē*) is a place of confinement, either for humans while living (not dead), as in a jail, or for evil spirits (BDAG 1067-68; TDNT 9:241-44). In Jewish and early Christian tradition, evil spirits are confined in a variety of locations, including in the earth (1 En. 10.4; 14.5; 15.8, 10; 67.7; Jub. 5.6; 2 Pet. 2:4; Jude 6; Rev. 20:3), in the heavens (2 En. 7.1-3; 18.3; Eph. 6:12), or at the end of both heaven and earth (1 En. 18.12-14; 21.1-10). The location meant here is uncertain, but

biblical and Second Temple Jewish literature. Why does Peter reference this event in the context of suffering for righteousness' sake? Scot McKnight puts it well: "Just as Jesus was vindicated before his opponents, so also will Christians be, if they, like Jesus, remain faithful and righteous to the tasks God has called them to do."[25]

Peter now turns to draw a connection between the imagery of the flood and baptism:

> …the ark was being prepared, in which a few, that is, eight persons, were brought safely through water. Baptism, which corresponds to this, now saves you, not as a removal of dirt from the body but as an appeal to God for a good conscience, through the resurrection of Jesus Christ.
> —1 Peter 3:20–21

According to Peter, baptism "corresponds to" the floodwaters. Just as the floodwaters brought deliverance for Noah and his family from a corrupt and violent world, baptism represents the believers' salvation from the fallen present world. We should note that Peter does not suggest that the ritual of baptism itself secures eternal salvation, as though the ritual alone were sufficient to "save." As Keener writes, "Rather than merely washing away dirt, deliberate Christian immersion signifies *the commitment of a conscience clear before God*."[26] Baptism is significant for believers because it signifies a salvation already made possible "through the resurrection of Jesus Christ" (1 Pet. 3:21).[27] Baptism visibly expresses

---

according to tradition the angels are to remain in confinement until they are destroyed at the consummation (Jude 6; 2 Pet. 2:4)."

25 McKnight, *1 Peter*, 217.
26 Keener, *1 Peter*, 283.
27 See Watson, "First Peter," 92: "Baptism is a pledge that the salvation wrought by the cross has become effective in the lives of believers."

the believers' pledge of commitment to the risen Messiah, who saves them.[28] As Keener writes, "Peter may be reminding believers facing suffering that their baptism has irrevocably committed them to Christ, as well as united them with Noah's deliverance and Christ's triumph."[29]

Peter concludes this section by declaring that the Messiah "has gone into heaven and is at the right hand of God, with angels, authorities, and powers having been subjected to him" (1 Pet. 3:22). According to Peter, Yeshua is seated at the right hand of God—a position that signifies supreme honor and authority. To sit at God's right hand is to be enthroned as ruler over all creation.[30] Yeshua has been granted all authority in heaven and on earth (Matt. 28:18), and even the "angels, authorities, and powers"—spiritual forces that often fight against God's people (1 Pet. 5:8; Eph. 6:12)—are under subjection to the Messiah (cf. Col. 2:15). Though circumstances are difficult, Peter reassures his readers of who truly reigns.

Lessons for Today: Hope Worth Defending

In 1 Peter 3:15, Peter instructs believers to always be ready to "make a defense" for their hope in the Messiah. Here, Peter uses the Greek term *apologia* (ἀπολογία), which is where we get our English word "apologetics." What is apologetics? Simply put, apologetics is the "rational defense of the Christian faith, its tenets and practices."[31] It is a field of theology focused on explaining and defending the truth claims of Christianity,

---

28 See Keener, *1 Peter*, 283: "If a pledge is in view here, it probably means a pledge to maintain a good conscience, whether as a pledge offered when undertaking baptism (perhaps in response to a question) or the pledge implicitly expressed by baptism itself."
29 Keener, *1 Peter*, 283.
30 Watson, "First Peter," 92.
31 Justo L. González, *Essential Theological Terms* (Louisville, KY: John Knox Press, 2005), 13.

fulfilling Peter's charge to be prepared to make a defense of our hope in the Messiah.

Today, many believers overlook the value of apologetics. Some even dismiss it entirely, calling it nothing more than intellectual brain candy and a distraction from the central commands to love God and our neighbor. Consequently, most modern churches neglect to teach apologetics. However, when done right, apologetics is far from a distraction. In fact, it serves as a powerful way to *walk out* our love for God and for our neighbor.

Aristotle once defined love as "wishing for anyone the things which we believe to be good, for his sake but not for our own, and procuring them for him as far as lies in our power" (*Rhetoric* 2.4).[32] I think Aristotle's definition of love toward others is accurate and reflects what we see in Scripture. For example, Philippians 2:4 calls believers to look not only to their own interests but also to the interests of others. If we claim to love our neighbor, we should want what is "good" for him and do what we can to provide it. And for human beings, the greatest good is knowing God and having a relationship with him. That is the very purpose of our existence (Eccles. 12:13). Apologetics plays a vital role in this pursuit. Providing strong arguments for our hope in God helps people wrestle with tough questions and doubts, clearing the way for faith. By removing obstacles to faith, apologetics opens the door for people to experience the greatest good: knowing and enjoying God for eternity.

This is why the apostle Paul frequently used apologetics in his own ministry. His goal was for both Jews and Gentiles to come to know the Messiah and be saved. Luke tells us that Paul regularly attended synagogue services on the Sabbath and "reasoned" with others from the Scriptures, "*explaining* and *proving* that it was necessary for the Christ to suffer and to rise from the dead, and saying, 'This Jesus, whom I proclaim to you,

---

32 Aristotle, *Aristotle in 23 Volumes*, vol. 22, trans. J. H. Freese (Cambridge, MA: Harvard University Press, 1926), n.p. This concept of love is later echoed by Thomas Aquinas (*Summa Theologiae*, I–II, q. 26, a. 4).

is the Christ'" (Acts 17:2–3, emphasis added). Paul's apologetic efforts were effective, as Luke notes that "some of them were persuaded" (Acts 17:4). Later in the same chapter, Paul reasons with Greek philosophers, and we see the same thing—he successfully persuades some of them (Acts 17:33). Paul's use of apologetics was an act of love for his neighbors. He sought their greatest good by guiding them toward a relationship with the Messiah.

In addition to loving non-believers by responding to their questions and leading them to the Messiah, apologetics also serves as a powerful way to love and encourage those who already believe. For instance, Luke introduces us to Apollos, a Jewish follower of Yeshua who was an eloquent speaker and well-versed in the Scriptures (Acts 18:24). After receiving more thorough instruction from Priscilla and Aquila (Acts 18:26), Apollos traveled to Achaia, where he "powerfully refuted" his opponents in public, using the Scriptures to prove that Yeshua is the Messiah. Significantly, Luke notes that Apollos's apologetic efforts "greatly helped" the other believers in the area (Acts 18:27–28). Apologetics is essential for strengthening the faith of believers, giving them the confidence that our beliefs are grounded in truth and supported by sound reasoning.

We have seen how apologetics helps us love our neighbor, but how does it help us love God? Yeshua taught that we are to love God not only with all our heart and soul, but also with all our mind (Matt. 22:37). Loving God with our mind involves seeking to grow in knowledge of God and his word. Engaging in apologetics keeps our faith from becoming intellectually shallow. Much like Jacob, who wrestled with God and refused to let go until he received a blessing, apologetics invites us to wrestle with difficult questions in pursuit of truth. And in that struggle, there is blessing. The journey of seeking answers, exploring Scripture, and overcoming doubts leads to spiritual growth and deep connection with God.

However, while studying apologetics is an important part of discipleship, like any good thing, it can be misused. Some may wield their knowledge to demean others or enter debates solely to boost their own ego by "winning" an argument, instead of engaging out of genuine love for God and neighbor. Peter was aware of this risk, which is why he included an important qualification in his call to make a defense of our hope: "yet do it with gentleness and respect" (1 Pet. 3:15). Apologetics must not be driven by self-interest. Instead, it must be guided by a spirit of gentleness and respect. Before presenting an argument for your beliefs, take a moment to consider your motivation. Also, pay attention to your tone and delivery. Are you being gracious and gentle, even as you point out weaknesses in someone's argument? Are you showing respect to the person, even though you strongly disagree with their views? If you are not engaging others with gentleness and respect, you are not practicing apologetics in the way Scripture calls us to. Pursuing apologetics properly involves not only becoming thoughtful and well-informed, but also kind and humble.

Our salvation is a hope worth defending, and apologetics equips us with the knowledge needed to boldly answer anyone who asks about this hope within us. It enables us to love our neighbors by clearing away obstacles to belief, helping them experience the greatest good: knowing and enjoying God for eternity. It also allows us to support fellow believers by strengthening their faith and addressing their doubts. Through apologetics, we fulfill the command to love God with our minds by deepening our understanding of him and his word. And because true apologetics requires not just knowledge but also gentleness and respect, it helps shape our character and grow in Messiah-like love.

Chapter 7

The End of All Things is At Hand
(1 Peter 4:1–11)

1 Since therefore Christ suffered in the flesh, arm yourselves with the same way of thinking, for whoever has suffered in the flesh has ceased from sin, **2** so as to live for the rest of the time in the flesh no longer for human passions but for the will of God. **3** For the time that is past suffices for doing what the Gentiles want to do, living in sensuality, passions, drunkenness, orgies, drinking parties, and lawless idolatry. **4** With respect to this they are surprised when you do not join them in the same flood of debauchery, and they malign you; **5** but they will give account to him who is ready to judge the living and the dead. **6** For this is why the gospel was preached even to those who are dead, that though judged in the flesh the way people are, they might live in the spirit the way God does.

7 The end of all things is at hand; therefore be self-controlled and sober-minded for the sake of your prayers. **8** Above all, keep loving one another earnestly, since love covers a multitude of sins. **9** Show hospitality to one another without grumbling. **10** As each has received a gift, use it to serve one another, as good stewards of God's varied grace: **11** whoever speaks, as one who speaks oracles of God; whoever serves, as one who serves by the strength that God supplies—in order that in everything God may be glorified through Jesus Christ. To him belong glory and dominion forever and ever. Amen.

The End of All Things is At Hand (1 Peter 4:1–11)

In this section of his epistle, Peter continues his teaching on how believers are to respond to suffering. He had just taught that it may be God's will for his people to endure undeserved suffering, pointing to Yeshua as the ultimate example of someone who suffered for righteousness' sake and was vindicated. Now, Peter calls believers to adopt the same mindset as Messiah: "Since therefore Christ suffered in the flesh, arm yourselves with the same way of thinking" (1 Pet. 4:1).

What does it mean to adopt the Messiah's "way of thinking" with regard to suffering? Believers must be mentally and spiritually prepared to endure suffering, just as the Messiah was. The Greek verb translated "arm yourselves" (ὁπλίζω) is commonly found in military contexts in ancient Greek literature, evoking imagery similar to Paul's exhortations to put on spiritual armor (2 Cor. 10:4; Eph. 6:10–20; 1 Thess. 5:8).[1] Just as soldiers equip themselves for battle, believers must equip themselves with the Messiah's "way of thinking"—one that accepts suffering for righteousness' sake as God's will and remains steadfast in the face of persecution. Peter adds, "whoever has suffered in the flesh has ceased from sin," meaning that those willing to suffer as followers of Yeshua reveal that they are no longer enslaved to sin. Their lives now reflect a break from former sinful patterns, as they choose to live "no longer for human passions but for the will of God" (1 Pet. 4:2).

Peter now turns to describe the types of sins his readers used to engage in before they became followers of the Messiah. He writes that "the time that is past suffices for doing what the Gentiles want to do" (1 Pet. 4:3). Essentially, Peter tells his readers that they have already spent more than enough time living as unbelievers. That old way of life—a life marked by sexual immorality, drunkenness, and idolatry—is no longer who they are. They have been "born again" into God's family (1 Pet. 1:3, 23), and their old way of life is now over.

---

1   Craig S. Keener, *1 Peter: A Commentary* (Grand Rapids: Baker Academic, 2021), 290.

The End of All Things is At Hand (1 Peter 4:1–11)

At this point, I should mention a Roman institution that was prevalent at this time: the imperial cult. This institution, which involved deifying emperors and members of their families, functioned to legitimize imperial authority and foster unity across the empire by intertwining political loyalty with religious worship. As Kelly D. Liebengood explains, the imperial cult was deeply embedded in the very fabric of public and social life:

> [T]he cult extended to every aspect of life. Roman imperial ideology permeated civic space through the design of city structures and even city design as a whole. Public institutions such as the agora, the bouleuterion, the gymnasium, and the baths tended to be associated with the imperial cult. Imperial honorary inscriptions were placed through the city landscape. What is more, imperial ideology was expressed through entertainment—the theater, festivals, and games all promoted Roman imperial worship, and some of the events would have lasted from several days to a week or more.[2]

For Peter's original readers, abandoning "what the Gentiles want to do" meant distancing themselves from the imperial cult. This required withdrawing "from nearly all public forms of celebration, entertainment, leisure, and community pride," which would have been seen by their neighbors as socially disruptive or even threatening.[3] Because of their exclusive devotion to the God of Israel, followers of Yeshua could no longer participate in many of the activities they once did. As a result, Peter notes that the "Gentiles" (unbelievers) are "surprised" that these believers no longer join them in their "flood of debauchery" and react with slander and insults (1 Pet. 4:4). This hostility is fueled by the fear

---

2 Kelly D. Liebengood, *Reading 1 Peter After Supersessionism: Jewish Apostolic Affirmation of Gentile Israelhood* (Eugene, OR: Cascade, 2025), 63.

3 Liebengood, *Reading 1 Peter*, 64.

The End of All Things is At Hand (1 Peter 4:1–11)

that the believers' refusal to take part in cultural activities might offend the gods and evoke their punishment. As Duane F. Watson writes, "Nonparticipation in the emperor cult could be considered treasonous, and forsaking observances to the gods was counted as exposing the population to divine wrath."[4]

Though his readers are experiencing hostility because of their commitment to the Messiah, Peter reminds them that God will ultimately judge every person. He writes that the unbelievers "will give account to him who is ready to judge the living and the dead" (1 Pet. 4:5). Therefore, believers need not agonize over the criticisms or hostility of unbelievers. One day, God will judge all people, past and present. No one will be exempt. On that day, those who remained faithful to the Lord despite suffering in this life will be fully vindicated.

Peter continues by saying, "For this is why the gospel was preached even to those who are dead, that though judged in the flesh the way people are, they might live in the spirit the way God does" (1 Pet. 4:6). Some interpret this verse to mean that Yeshua preached to human souls in Hades—the abode of the dead—during the time between his crucifixion and resurrection. They connect this verse to 1 Peter 3:19, where Peter says that Yeshua preached "to the spirits in prison." However, as discussed in the previous chapter, I think that interpretation is unlikely. Craig S. Keener offers a helpful summary of what Peter is most likely conveying in this passage:

> Traditionally, many believed that the point was that Jesus preached to the dead in Hades. This approach fits the traditional view of 3:19-20, which does appear in the fairly near context. A majority of scholars today, however, understand the verse as referring to the gospel being preached to those who are now

---

4 Duane F. Watson, "First Peter," in *First and Second Peter*, by Duane F. Watson and Terrance Callan, PCNT (Grand Rapids: Baker Academic, 2012), 98.

dead (but were alive when the gospel was preached to them; cf. 1:25). On this latter interpretation, those who have been martyred by human judges will ultimately be vindicated and raised from the dead, because God is the one who will judge ultimately (cf. 4:5).[5]

In other words, this verse is not suggesting that the gospel was preached to people while they were dead. Rather, it refers to individuals who heard the gospel during their lifetime, believed it, and as a result, faced persecution and ultimately died. However, the very gospel that led to them being "judged in the flesh" will also lead to their victory. They will "live in the spirit," meaning they will be raised from the dead. This parallels what Peter says about Yeshua, who was "put to death in the flesh but made alive in the Spirit" (1 Pet. 3:18).[6] As Scot McKnight writes, "Those who hear the gospel and respond, even if they are killed for their faith, will be vindicated ultimately before God."[7]

Peter continues by announcing, "the end of all things is at hand" (1 Pet. 4:7). Like Yeshua, James, Paul, and others, Peter spoke of the end of the age as though it were imminent (cf. Luke 21:36; James 5:8; Phil. 4:5). The New Testament writers understood Yeshua's first coming as the beginning of the eschatological era—the "last days"—which will ultimately be fulfilled at his return. In that sense, we have been living in the "last days" for the past 2,000 years. While that may seem like a long time

---

5 Keener, *1 Peter*, 309.
6 See Thomas R. Schreiner: "The contrast between 'flesh' and 'spirit' here is parallel to 1 Pet 3:18 since Christ also died in terms of his flesh but was raised to life by the Holy Spirit. A similar destiny awaits believers. They die physically but will be raised to life by the Holy Spirit. I am suggesting, therefore, that Peter does not consider the intermediate state here but the resurrection of the dead. He uses the present tense because the future will certainly come to pass. Peter reminds his readers that even if they die physically, death is not ultimate. The resurrection awaits them" (*1, 2 Peter, Jude*, NAC [Nashville: B&H Publishing, 2003], 209).
7 Scot McKnight, *1 Peter*, NIVAC (Grand Rapids: Zondervan, 1996), 228.

The End of All Things is At Hand (1 Peter 4:1–11)

from our human perspective, Peter does say in his second epistle that for the Lord, "a day is like a thousand years" (2 Pet. 3:8–9). What appears to be a lengthy period of time from a human perspective is merely a fleeting moment from God's perspective.

In any case, in light of the end being "at hand," Peter urges his readers to remain "self-controlled and sober-minded" (1 Pet. 4:7). These instructions echo themes he introduced earlier in his letter (1 Pet. 1:13). To be sober-minded means maintaining mental discipline—that is, refusing to let worldly distractions derail your focus. Instead, Peter wants his readers to stay centered on their calling and responsibilities as disciples of Yeshua. Peter mentions that being self-controlled and sober-minded is essential "for the sake of your prayers" (1 Pet. 4:7). In the previous chapter, he already pointed out that a believer's behavior can affect whether their prayers are heard (1 Pet. 3:7, 12).[8] This principle is also found throughout the Hebrew Scriptures (cf. Jer. 7:16; 14:12; Ezek. 8:18; Zech. 7:13; Prov. 15:8; 28:9). With "the end of all things" approaching, Peter urges his readers to live rightly so that their prayers remain effective and unhindered.

In addition to being self-controlled and sober-minded, Peter instructs his readers, "Above all, keep loving one another earnestly, since love covers a multitude of sins" (1 Pet. 4:8). Peter places great emphasis on his readers loving one another. It is what he urges them to do "above all" else. In the midst of persecution, it is crucial for the community to support, encourage, and comfort one another. And this love is not to be passive; they must love one another "earnestly." As McKnight observes, "Since familial, business, and social relationships tend to become frayed and tested when difficulties arise, Peter urges them to love one another

---

8   See Watson, "First Peter," 102: "in light of other references to prayer (3:7, 12), right conduct is needed for prayers to be effective, something quite necessary when the end and judgment are imminent."

with great effort because he knows how much work it takes with the dark cloud of persecution and stress hovering above."[9]

According to Peter, such love "covers a multitude of sins" (1 Pet. 4:8). Here, Peter draws from Proverbs 10:12. Peter's point seems to be that those who truly love will be quick to forgive, choosing to "cover" the faults and offenses of others. Such a willingness to forgive and cover offenses is essential for the believing community if they are to glorify God (1 Pet. 4:11). Equally important is Peter's instruction to show "hospitality to one another without grumbling" (1 Pet. 4:9). His hope is that believers will care for each other sincerely and offer help out of genuine love. During difficult times, when resources are stretched thin, it is easy to become irritated or reluctant to share, which perhaps is why Peter emphasizes doing so "without grumbling."[10] In challenging seasons, believers are called to support one another willingly, not treat each other as burdens.

Peter continues: "As each has received a gift, use it to serve one another, as good stewards of God's varied grace" (1 Pet. 4:10). The Greek word for "gift" here is charisma (χάρισμα), which suggests that Peter is referring to spiritual gifts such as prophecy, encouragement, and other God-given abilities bestowed on each believer. As Keener writes:

> The Greek term translated as "gift" here, *charisma*, was still rare in this period, so it is probably no coincidence that Paul uses the term in a similar way (esp. in Rom. 12:6; 1 Cor. 1:7; 12:4, 9, 28–31; cf. 1 Tim. 4:14; 2 Tim. 1:6; possibly also Rom. 1:11), suggesting a wider early Christian usage. The prophetic element in 1 Pet. 4:11 is another indication that we may read Peter's use of the term *charisma* in the light of wider early Christian usage; prophecy is one of the few gifts invariably among Paul's lists

---

9   McKnight, *1 Peter*, 237–238.
10 Watson, "First Peter," 103.

> of *charismata*. Both Peter and Paul use *charisma* in connection with *charis*, "grace" (Rom. 12:6; cf. Rom. 5:15; Eph. 4:7); God's generous benevolence not only rescues us, but equips us to be his agents in gifts for one another. God has graced each of us with different gifts and therefore we can use these to serve one another. We must share these gifts, since God gave them to us for the church as a whole (Rom. 12:4–8; 1 Cor. 12:7; Eph. 4:11–12). The many-sided character of the grace reinforces the idea that God uses different individuals in different ways, but it is the same God working through all of them (cf. 1 Cor. 12:4-6, 11).[11]

As Keener suggests, Peter's reference to "one who speaks oracles of God" (1 Pet. 4:11) likely alludes to the gift of prophecy. Much like Paul, Peter emphasizes that such gifts are not for personal gain but are meant to be used in service to one another, "in order that in everything God may be glorified through Jesus Christ." For Peter, the ultimate goal and purpose of everything believers do is to bring glory to God. In that spirit, he concludes this passage with a doxology, a liturgical expression of praise: "To him belong glory and dominion forever and ever. Amen" (1 Pet. 4:11).

Lessons for Today: Leave the Past Behind

When we put our faith in Yeshua as Messiah and Lord, we are "born again" into God's family and receive a new identity, purpose, and hope. However, entering this new life means letting go of the old one. The former "you" must be put to death. And turning away from past behaviors and toward a life of holiness will impact your relationships with people who were part

---

11   Keener, *1 Peter*, 323.

The End of All Things is At Hand (1 Peter 4:1–11)

of your old life. As Peter writes, "they are surprised when you do not join them" in the things you used to do (1 Pet. 4:4). Although you have found a new life full of purpose, hope, and joy, many will not welcome the change.

Just a few years after Peter wrote his first epistle, followers of Yeshua were subjected to government-sanctioned imprisonment, torture, and even execution. As Joseph M. Bryant notes, under Nero's rule, "the mere fact of 'being a Christian' was sufficient for state officials to impose capital punishment."[12] Without question, believers in the modern Western world have it quite easy compared to Peter's original audience in the first century. (Of course, the same cannot be said for Christians in China and certain Muslim-majority nations, and we must remain diligent in praying for and supporting our brothers and sisters in those hostile places.) While we can be grateful for the relative tolerance Christians experience in the West, we should still not be surprised when we inevitably face opposition, rejection, and misunderstanding (1 Pet. 4:12). Even if that opposition does not come from the government, broader society still often rejects the values we hold regarding things like life, marriage, sex, and more. When we adopt the Messiah's "way of thinking" (1 Pet. 4:1) on such matters, it is bound to clash with the values of the world. What makes this especially difficult is that the "world" often consists of old friends and family members whom we still love deeply.

As those who have been born again into God's family, we are called to live the rest of our lives "no longer for human passions but for the will of God" (1 Pet. 4:2). Though the eternal reward of following Yeshua is immeasurable, it comes at the cost of leaving our old way of life behind. Many of us remember the moment we chose to follow Yeshua and turned away from the "passions" we once pursued. Walking in holiness, aligning our lives with God's word, and encountering his presence through prayer and worship brought freedom and blessing to our lives, but it also shook

---

12 Joseph M. Bryant, "The Sect-Church Dynamic and Christian Expansion in the Roman Empire: Persecution, Penitential Discipline, and Schism in Sociological Perspective, BJS 44, no. 2 (1993), 313–314.

The End of All Things is At Hand (1 Peter 4:1–11)

the people around us. Some friends and family members perhaps felt judged and questioned whether we were becoming "too extreme." Some quietly pulled away while others openly criticized us. While we did not face physical persecution, the emotional sting of rejection was real. And sadly, for us as Messianic believers, that pain is often felt twice over: when we begin to embrace aspects of the Torah such as keeping the Sabbath and avoiding unclean foods, we not only encounter pushback from the wider world but also from many beloved fellow Christians who don't share those convictions. In addition, Messianic Jews often experience rejection from their own Jewish family members who do not share their faith in Yeshua.

As difficult as it may be, in order to endure our earthy sojourn as believers, like Paul, we must stop seeking man's approval (Gal. 1:10). That is part of what it means to "arm yourselves with the same way of thinking" as the Messiah (1 Pet. 4:1). The Messiah lived his life on earth fully committed to doing the will of his Father, regardless of the cost. He not only suffered physically but also emotionally. He was misunderstood, betrayed, falsely accused, and rejected. Yet he endured it all because his focus was not on pleasing people but on doing his Father's will. Arming ourselves with his way of thinking means preparing for battle. The mental and emotional fight will be real and intense, but the reward of knowing the Messiah makes every battle worth it. When you let go of your old life, you may lose comfort, security, and even close relationships, but you gain something far greater.

How can we practically endure the trials that come with our new life in the Messiah? Two points come to mind. First, we must stay connected to other believers. This is why Peter urges his readers to love one another earnestly, to offer hospitality without grumbling, and to use their spiritual gifts to serve one another (1 Pet. 4:8–11). Leaving behind your old life can feel lonely, but God has given us the Body of Messiah as a source of love, support, and encouragement during our time as resident aliens in this world. Second, we are called to respond to reviling with blessing (1

The End of All Things is At Hand (1 Peter 4:1–11)

Pet. 3:9). Despite our disagreements, we should seek to honor, bless, and pray for those who insult or oppose us. Holiness often invites hostility, but our love, good deeds, and prayers may cause others to reflect on their own lives and even draw them toward Yeshua (1 Pet. 2:12), or at the very least, open the door to peace (1 Pet. 3:13).

Stand firm and live to do God's will. After all, "The end of all things is at hand" (1 Pet. 4:7). The pain of rejection is temporary, but the overwhelming joy of knowing the Messiah lasts for eternity.

Chapter 8

Persevere through Suffering
(1 Peter 4:12–19)

> **12** Beloved, do not be surprised at the fiery trial when it comes upon you to test you, as though something strange were happening to you. **13** But rejoice insofar as you share Christ's sufferings, that you may also rejoice and be glad when his glory is revealed. **14** If you are insulted for the name of Christ, you are blessed, because the Spirit of glory and of God rests upon you. **15** But let none of you suffer as a murderer or a thief or an evildoer or as a meddler. **16** Yet if anyone suffers as a Christian, let him not be ashamed, but let him glorify God in that name. **17** For it is time for judgment to begin at the household of God; and if it begins with us, what will be the outcome for those who do not obey the gospel of God? **18** And "If the righteous is scarcely saved, what will become of the ungodly and the sinner?" **19** Therefore let those who suffer according to God's will entrust their souls to a faithful Creator while doing good.

After urging his readers to leave behind their former way of life, love one another earnestly, and faithfully use their gifts for God's glory (1 Pet. 4:1–11), Peter now encourages them not to be caught off guard by the trials that inevitably accompany a life devoted to following Yeshua: "Beloved, do not be surprised at the fiery trial when it comes upon you to test you, as though something strange were happening to you" (1 Pet. 4:12). Since the Messiah suffered, believers should expect that following him will lead to suffering in their own lives. After all, that is precisely what Yeshua promised (John 15:18–21; 16:33).

Persevere through Suffering (1 Peter 4:12–19)

What does Peter mean by "fiery trial"? Many have understood this to be a reference to the brutal persecution Christians experienced under Nero,[1] but that is unlikely since 1 Peter was written before those events took place (see "Authorship" and "Date" in the Introduction). It is more likely that Peter is referring to the image of a furnace used to test and refine gold, echoing the metaphor he used earlier in the letter: "so that the tested genuineness of your faith—more precious than gold that perishes though it is tested by fire—may be found to result in praise and glory and honor at the revelation of Jesus Christ" (1 Pet. 1:7).[2] According to Peter, these fiery trials are designed to "test" believers, refining them, much like fire purifies gold. As they endure these trials, Peter instructs his readers to "rejoice insofar as you share Christ's sufferings, that you may also rejoice and be glad when his glory is revealed" (1 Pet. 4:13). When believers suffer for righteousness' sake, they are following in the footsteps of the Messiah (1 Pet. 2:21). Therefore, they can rejoice in the hope that, when Yeshua's glory is revealed, they will share in that glory, just as they currently share in his suffering (1 Pet. 1:3–5).[3] Also, just like gold shines brightly after it has been purified and refined, so too will God's people (e.g., Dan. 12:2–3; Isa. 60:1–3). As Paul also writes, "The spirit himself bears witness with our spirit that we are children of God, and if children, then heirs—heirs of God and fellow heirs with Christ, provided we suffer with him in order

---

1 Karen H. Jobes, *1 Peter*, BECNT (Grand Rapids: Zondervan, 2005), 9. Jobes cites John A. T. Robinson, *Redating the New Testament* (Philadelphia: Westminster, 1976), 159.
2 Craig S. Keener, *1 Peter: A Commentary* (Grand Rapids: Baker Academic, 2021), 334. Keener adds: "The Didache, in the late first or possibly early second century, applies it to the period of final tribulation and testing before Christ's return (*Did.* 16:5). See also Paul J. Achtemeier: "The reference to the events as a πύρωσις ("burning") probably owes less to the punishment inflicted on Christians in Rome by Nero than it does to the biblical metaphor of a purifying and proving fire, often with eschatological overtones, a metaphor already employed by our author in 1:7" (*1 Peter*, Hermeneia [Minneapolis: Fortress Press, 1996], 305–306).
3 See Keener, *1 Peter*, 335: "Those whose suffering shares in Christ's sufferings (cf. Phil. 3:10) can rejoice, because they will also share his glory."

that we may also be glorified with him" (Rom. 8:16–17). Finding joy in suffering because of a future glory is a consistent theme throughout both the Hebrew Scriptures (e.g., Dan. 12:1–3; Joel 2) and the New Testament (e.g., Matt. 5:10–12; 10:22; Rom. 8:17; Phil. 3:10–11; James 1:12).[4]

Peter continues by encouraging his readers that if they are "insulted for the name of Christ," they are actually "blessed" (1 Pet. 4:14; cf. Matt. 5:11–12). Why? Because, as Peter explains, "the Spirit of glory and of God rests upon [them]" (1 Pet. 4:14). The image of the Spirit "resting" upon believers alludes to Isaiah 11:2, which speaks of the Spirit of the LORD resting upon the Messiah (cf. Matt. 3:16).[5] Peter is assuring his readers that this same Spirit of God now rests upon them. Even in the midst of suffering, believers experience the presence of the Holy Spirit, who comforts them and serves as a guarantee of the glory yet to come. As Paul writes, God has prepared us for a "heavenly dwelling," and "has given us the Spirit as a guarantee" while we wait (2 Cor. 5:2, 5).

While believers can expect to suffer, Peter warns that not all suffering brings glory to God, particularly the suffering that results from sinful conduct: "But let none of you suffer as a murderer or a thief or an evildoer or as a meddler" (1 Pet. 4:15). As Peter has repeatedly stressed, believers are called to suffer for doing good, not for doing evil (1 Pet. 2:20; 3:17). The Torah explicitly prohibits murder and theft (Exod. 20:13, 15), and Peter admonishes believers to maintain "holy" conduct consistent with those standards, even in the midst of suffering (1 Pet. 1:14–16). Craig S. Keener notes that the term κακοποιός ("evildoer") in this specific form appears only in 1 Peter "and reminds readers to avoid giving any substance to the slanders against them (1 Pet. 2:12, 14; cf. the verb in 3:17)."[6] The meaning of the final term, ἀλλοτριεπίσκοπος ("meddler"), is debated. As Paul J. Achtemeier explains, "The two components of the

---

4 Achtemeier, *1 Peter*, 306–307.
5 Duane F. Watson, "First Peter," in *First and Second Peter*, by Duane F. Watson and Terrance Callan, PCNT (Grand Rapids: Baker Academic, 2012), 111.
6 Keener, *1 Peter*, 340.

word would mean someone who was involved in overseeing (επισκοπος) the affairs of someone else (αλλοτριος), which in turn could mean anything from a moral or social busybody to a revolutionary to someone who, charged with overseeing another's goods, embezzles them."[7] Achtemeier favors the last option, concluding that "ἀλλοτριεπίσκοπος ought here to be understood with the first three as implying illegal activity, that is, as embezzlement of the goods of another, even though the word may, like κακοποιός ["evildoer"], have a range not limited to acts punishable by law."[8] In any case, in line with Peter's earlier exhortations to behave honorably among the Gentiles (1 Pet. 2:11–12), if believers must suffer, let it be for doing good so that God is glorified in it.

In contrast to the type of suffering that does not glorify God, Peter writes, "Yet if anyone suffers as a Christian, let him not be ashamed but let him glorify God in that name" (1 Pet. 4:16). Believers do not need to fear being scorned for their beliefs and values, because God has promised that "whoever believes in him will not be put to shame" (1 Pet. 2:6; cf. Phil. 1:20).[9] The Greek word Χριστιανός ("Christian") simply means "one who is associated with Christ."[10] The term appears only three times in the New Testament, with the other two occurrences found in Acts, where it is used by unbelievers (Acts 11:26; 26:28). In the first century, the term carried a negative connotation.[11] Yet Peter urges his readers not to be ashamed of carrying that name. Early believers apparently took this

---

7   Achtemeier, *1 Peter*, 310. See also Keener, 1 Peter, 340–341; Watson, "1 Peter," 111.
8   Achtemeier, *1 Peter*, 310–311.
9   Watson, "First Peter," 111. See also Keener, *1 Peter*, 341: "Others might ridicule one as a Christian, trying to shame one; but this is an opportunity to honor God; in the end, God will remove the shame and vindicate his servants."
10 BDAG, 971.
11 Watson, "First Peter," 111. Keener notes that a graffito from Pompeii, dated between 62 and 79 CE, uses the term to mock followers of the Messiah. He also notes that being a "Christian" was "a temporarily chargeable offense under Nero, and Roman governors continued to apply the term to the group in legal settings in the early second century" (*1 Peter*, 345).

to heart, and by the early second century, followers of the Messiah widely adopted the name for themselves.[12]

Why should believers expect to suffer? As Peter explains, "For it is time for judgment to begin with the household of God" (1 Pet. 4:17). God has begun to judge, and God uses suffering as a form of loving discipline to refine the faith of those who belong to his household (1 Pet. 1:6–7; cf. Heb. 12:7; 1 Cor. 11:29–31).[13] Peter then warns that those who reject the Gospel will face far more severe consequences in the end: "and if it begins with us, what will be the outcome for those who do not obey the gospel of God?" (1 Pet. 4:17). If even God's own children undergo judgment, how much greater will the judgment be for those who do not belong to him? To underscore this point, Peter cites Proverbs 11:31: "If the righteous is scarcely saved, what will become of the ungodly and the sinner?" (1 Pet. 4:18) In other words, if the faithful face trials now, the fate of the unbelieving on the day of judgment will be far more terrifying.

Peter closes this section with an exhortation: "Therefore let those who suffer according to God's will entrust their souls to a faithful Creator while doing good." According to Peter, at times, it is indeed "God's will" for believers to suffer. Earlier, Peter explained that such suffering can glorify God since it serves as a witness to believers' hope in the Messiah (1 Pet. 3:14–16) and refines their faith (1 Pet. 1:6–7; 4:17). For this reason, believers must be ready to endure hardship while continuing to live righteously, fully entrusting themselves to their faithful Creator, who has promised to vindicate them (1 Pet. 4:13; 5:10).

---

12 The term is used in *Didache* 12.4; Ignatius, *Ephesians* 11.2; *Magnesians* 4; *Romans* 3.2. See Achtemeier, *1 Peter*, 313.
13 Keener, *1 Peter*, 347.

Persevere through Suffering (1 Peter 4:12–19)

Lessons for Today: The Benefits of Suffering

It is often claimed that God's will is for you to be successful, healthy, and wealthy in this life. Peter, however, teaches that it is "God's will" that you suffer for living righteously (1 Pet. 4:19). The apostle Paul echoes this teaching: "Indeed, all who desire to live a godly life in Christ Jesus will be persecuted" (2 Tim. 3:12). If God's entire plan for you was to be materially satisfied in this world, then your suffering would be a hindrance to that plan. But God's plans go beyond the material comforts of this world. We were not created in order to be comfortable, but rather to fear God and keep his commandments (Eccles. 12:13–14), bringing him glory in every circumstance. Suffering is one of the tools God uses to help us fulfill that purpose.

But what good can possibly come from suffering? How exactly can it help us fulfill God's purpose for us? For one thing, as Peter says, suffering tests and refines our faith. It leads to spiritual growth, teaching us obedience and imparting wisdom. James too reminds us that trials produce steadfastness, ultimately making us "perfect and complete, lacking in nothing" (James 1:4). Sometimes, suffering serves to break the grip of sin in our lives, making us less inclined to return to destructive patterns of behavior. As the psalmist proclaims, "Before I was afflicted I went astray, *but now* I keep your word" (Ps. 119:67, emphasis added). In this way, suffering helps us grow in wisdom and maturity. Though we may not always understand its purpose in the moment, we can rest in the promise that "God works all things together for good, for those who are called according to his purpose" (Rom. 8:28).

Another way suffering works for our good is that it strengthens community. Shared experiences of pain often create deep bonds with others. This is the foundation of support groups for those who have lost a loved one or are battling serious illness. There is a unique and strong connection that forms when people walk through hardship together. Similarly, when believers suffer for their faith, it fosters greater unity, love, and solidarity within the body of Messiah. This is why, in the midst of their suffering, Peter admonishes his readers, "Above all, keep loving one another earnestly" (1 Pet. 4:8). Peter even describes this kind of suffering as sharing in the sufferings of the Messiah (1 Pet. 4:13). Just as shared suffering draws us closer to one another, it can also deepen our intimacy with Yeshua. As the Psalmist reminds us, "The LORD is near to the brokenhearted" (Ps. 34:18). As Corrie Ten Boom, a Christian Holocaust survivor, wrote, "There is no pit so deep that God's love is not deeper still."[14] In our deepest pit of sorrow and pain, we can draw closer to God in a profound way.

However, while we acknowledge the ways God uses suffering for our good, we must also remember that we have been born again to a living hope (1 Pet. 1:3). Our present suffering is not the end of the story. One day, Yeshua will return, and all death, sorrow, tears, and pain will be abolished forever (Rev. 21:4). The inheritance awaiting God's children is so glorious that Paul describes our present trials as a "light momentary affliction" in comparison (2 Cor. 4:16–18). Even if we suffer throughout our entire lives, a time will come when all that pain will seem almost insignificant. After a million years of joy in God's eternal kingdom, the 70 or 80 years of earthly suffering will feel like a brief and distant memory.

Therefore, stay faithful in the midst of suffering, trusting that these trials are not without purpose. They are refining your faith and drawing you closer to God. And in the end, they are preparing you for a joy that is everlasting, far outweighing the pain of the present.

---

14 Corrie Ten Boom, *The Hiding Place* (Grand Rapids: Baker Publishing Group, 2006), 8.

Chapter 9

Clothe Yourselves with Humility
(1 Peter 5:1–5)

> **1** So I exhort the elders among you, as a fellow elder and a witness of the sufferings of Christ, as well as a partaker in the glory that is going to be revealed: **2** shepherd the flock of God that is among you, exercising oversight, not under compulsion, but willingly, as God would have you; not for shameful gain, but eagerly; **3** not domineering over those in your charge, but being examples to the flock. **4** And when the chief Shepherd appears, you will receive the unfading crown of glory. **5** Likewise, you who are younger, be subject to the elders. Clothe yourselves, all of you, with humility toward one another, for "God opposes the proud but gives grace to the humble."

In chapter 4 of his epistle, Peter exhorted believers not to be ashamed of suffering as Christians, but to see it as a means of sharing in Messiah's sufferings and glorifying God. He reminded them that judgment begins with the household of God and encouraged them to entrust themselves to their faithful Creator while continuing to do good. Now, in 1 Peter 5:1–5, Peter turns his attention to the leaders of the community, urging them to shepherd God's flock with humility and integrity, while calling all believers to relate to one another with mutual humility and respect.

Peter opens his exhortation to "the elders" by pointing out three qualities that he has in common with them, the first being that he is a "fellow elder" (1 Pet. 5:1). Although Peter holds greater authority as an apostle (1 Pet. 1:1), he chooses to appeal to these elders as a friend and fellow servant. According to Scot McKnight, "While it may be argued that Peter condescends to their level, it is more likely that he is elevating their ministries and incorporating their work into his."[1]

What does Peter mean by "elder"? The word πρεσβύτερος ("elder") can refer either to an older individual or to someone in a position of leadership (e.g., Titus 1:5–6; James 5:14). In this context, the term clearly denotes a leadership role.[2] That said, the two ideas are connected, as the older men in the community often naturally held positions of authority and influence.[3] Additionally, the use of this term for a leadership role was likely adopted from Jewish tradition. As Craig Keener explains:

> Given the church's adaptation of synagogue models already effective in Diaspora cities, it is reasonable that they borrowed the title "elders" from there as well…Scholars note the widespread evidence for this office in the Jewish Diaspora. Usually a council of elders rather than a single elder exercised their activities in synagogues. That they appear in 1QS 6.8–9 [Dead Sea Scrolls] reinforces the impression that the Jewish usage was widespread.[4]

Elders functioned as spiritual leaders who were responsible for teaching sound doctrine, offering pastoral guidance, and ensuring the unity of the communities (1 Tim. 3:1–7; Titus 1:5–9). By calling himself a "fellow elder," Peter shows that he can relate to the burden of leadership these men are experiencing. He understands the pressure, stress, and responsibility that come with the role.

A second way that Peter identifies with these leaders is as "a witness of the sufferings of Christ" (1 Pet. 5:1). When he says "witness," Peter does not mean that he and these elders personally saw the Messiah crucified.

---

1 Scot McKnight, *1 Peter*, NIVAC (Grand Rapids: Zondervan, 1996), 259.
2 Duane F. Watson, "First Peter," in *First and Second Peter*, by Duane F. Watson and Terrance Callan, PCNT (Grand Rapids: Baker Academic, 2012), 116.
3 Craig S. Keener, *1 Peter: A Commentary* (Grand Rapids: Baker Academic, 2021), 355.
4 Keener, *1 Peter*, 356–357.

Rather, he means that both he and these elders bear witness to the gospel, the message of the suffering of Messiah for redemption. In this way, Peter and the elders are alike in their responsibility to proclaim and uphold that gospel. As Duane F. Watson writes:

> [W]hile Peter saw the daily suffering of Jesus, he was not an eyewitness to the interrogation or crucifixion of Jesus, having deserted Jesus with the other apostles (Mark 14:27, 50). If eyewitness of is the reference, the focus is on the author and the elders as joint witnesses to the suffering of Christ by preaching the gospel. Suffering is the central topic of this letter's witness (1:11; 2:21, 23–24; 3:18; 4:1, 13), and the portrayal of Peter in the NT is one of witness to the gospel, especially in the speeches and responses attributed to him in Acts (2:14–36 [v. 32]; 3:12–26 [v. 15]; 4:8–12; 5:30–32; 10:34–43 [vv. 39–41].[5]

The third way Peter identifies with these leaders is as "a partaker in the glory that is going to be revealed," highlighting the shared hope he holds with these elders—the same living hope into which all believers have been born through Yeshua's death and resurrection (1 Pet. 1:3–9). One day, the Messiah, the "chief Shepherd" (1 Pet. 5:4), will be revealed, and all God's people will share in the glory of his eternal kingdom.

Peter urges the elders to "shepherd the flock of God that is among you" (1 Pet. 5:2). Throughout Scripture, the image of a "shepherd" is often used to describe spiritual leaders (Jer. 23:4; Matt. 18:12–14; Acts 20:28; Eph. 4:11).[6] Just as Yeshua once commanded Peter to tend his sheep (John 21:15–17), Peter now calls these elders to faithfully tend God's sheep. Peter instructs the elders to carry out their leadership by "exercising oversight, not under compulsion, but willingly, as God would

---

5   Watson, "First Peter," 116.
6   Watson, "1 Peter," 117.

Clothe Yourselves with Humility (1 Peter 5:1–5)

have you." In other words, they are to watch over the flock entrusted to them—not out of mere obligation, but with a willing and eager heart, aligned with God's desires.[7] Elders need to sincerely care about the people they watch over. Their service must be free from selfish motives or the pursuit of "shameful gain" (cf. 1 Tim. 3:3, 8; Titus 1:7). Moreover, elders are not to be "domineering over those in [their] charge" (1 Pet. 5:3). Echoing Yeshua's teaching on servant leadership (Matt 20:25; Mark 10:42), Peter warns against using authority to control or intimidate.[8] Instead, elders are to lead with humility, setting an "example" through godly conduct.

Peter concludes his appeal to the elders by reminding them that "when the chief Shepherd appears, [they] will receive the unfading crown of glory" (1 Pet. 5:4). Though elders serve as shepherds, they do so under the authority of the chief Shepherd, Yeshua, and the flock ultimately belongs to God (1 Pet. 5:2). When Yeshua returns, faithful elders will be rewarded with a crown of glory (cf. 2 Tim. 4:8; James 1:12). In the ancient world, athletes were awarded crowns made of leaves as symbols of honor for their victories.[9] But unlike those perishable crowns, the reward for faithful service in God's kingdom is eternal and unfading. Peter may also be alluding to Proverbs 16:31, where gray hair is described as a "crown of glory," representing the honor gained through a righteous life.

Peter now shifts his attention from the elders to the younger members of the community, instructing them, "Likewise, you who are younger, be subject to the elders" (1 Pet. 5:5). Just as the elders are called to lead with humility, the younger believers are called to respond with humility through respectful submission. As noted above, those advanced in age often served as community leaders, and Scripture repeatedly emphasizes

---

7   Watson, "1 Peter," 117. See also McKnight, *1 Peter*, 261.
8   See Keener, *1 Peter*, 370: "Instead of leading by fiat, the elders could lead by example, by being a *role model*. Rather than compelling submission, they could (ideally) make resistance unnecessary, making submission and humility honorable."
9   Keener, *1 Peter*, 371–372. See also Watson, "First Peter," 118.

honoring the elderly (Lev. 19:32; 1 Tim. 5:1–2). Age is frequently associated with wisdom (Prov, 16:31; Job 12:12; 32:7). Therefore, younger believers are urged to "be subject" to their elders, showing respect for their authority, valuing their insight, and willingly following their guidance.[10]

In the end, regardless of age or position, Peter calls on *everyone* ("all of you") to "clothe yourselves with humility toward one another." Earlier, he urged the community to "put away" sinful attitudes like malice, deceit, and slander (1 Pet. 2:1), evoking the image of taking off a garment. Now, he encourages them to *put on* humility, clothing themselves with it.[11] To reinforce this command, Peter cites Proverbs 3:34: "God opposes the proud but gives grace to the humble." God resists those who do evil, but responds to humility with favor (1 Pet. 3:7, 12).

Lessons for Today: Honor Your Elders

Peter exhorts young believers to "be subject to the elders" (1 Pet. 5:5), a principle repeated throughout the New Testament (1 Tim. 5:1–2, 17–19; Heb. 13:17). This expectation to honor elders ultimately derives from the Torah, which states, "You shall stand up before the gray head and honor the face of an old man, and you shall fear your God: I am the LORD" (Lev. 19:32).

In Leviticus 19:32, the terms שֵׂיבָה ("gray head") and זָקֵן ("old man") both refer to old age.[12] Notably, זָקֵן also conveys the idea of an "elder"

---

10 See Watson, "First Peter," 118: "The same verb for 'be subject' (*hypotassō*) was used previously to describe the Christian attitude to human institutions, slaves to masters, and wives to husbands (2:13, 18; 3:1, 5); it denotes proper respect for authority and experience."
11 Keener, *1 Peter*, 377.
12 TWOT, 249. See, e.g., Gen. 24:1; Josh. 13:1.

Clothe Yourselves with Humility (1 Peter 5:1–5)

in the sense of a community leader or judge.[13] As noted above, this connection makes sense, as older individuals in the community naturally held positions of leadership and authority due to their wisdom and experience (Job 12:12; 32:7). The verse contains three commands: the first is to "stand up before the gray head." In the ancient world, rising when someone entered a room was a gesture of respect and honor, which ties directly into the second command: "honor" the elderly. By standing in their presence, one demonstrated recognition of their wisdom and esteemed position within the community.[14] The third commandment, "fear your God," directly connects honoring elders with revering God himself. The way we treat those whom God has endowed with wisdom and authority reflects the depth of our respect for the one who gave the commandment. In fact, the prophets regard young people disrespecting their elders as a sign that society has turned away from God and is on the verge of collapse (Isa. 3:5; Lam. 5:12).

Is the way we treat our elders today aligned with God's commandments? Do we recognize and value the wisdom that comes with age? Are we intentional about showing honor and respect to those who have gone before us? Sadly, in today's culture, old age is often not met with the honor and respect it deserves. Older people are frequently viewed as out of touch and not worthy of our attention. This perspective not only shows a lack of love and care for our older neighbors, but it also does a massive disservice to younger generations. Young people who regard older people as wise and authoritative can benefit from their life experience. But without the experience and insight of those who have gone before us, we are left to navigate life through trial and error, often learning important lessons only after costly mistakes.

We need to return to the biblical principle of honoring our elders. But how can we live this out today? What does honoring our elders look

---

13   TWOT, 249–250.
14   Jay Sklar, *Leviticus*, ZECOT (Grand Rapids: Zondervan, 2023), 542–543.

like in our modern culture? The Hebrew verb הָדַר ("honor") means "to show respect" or "to prefer."[15] In essence, honoring our elders means treating them with respect and esteeming them as valuable sources of wisdom. We should generally "prefer" their insight to that of our peers or those younger than us. This is a proper expression of humility (1 Pet. 5:5), "since in doing so we acknowledge that they have gained much wisdom over the years."[16] Honoring our elders does not mean we must agree with them on every issue. For instance, Paul acknowledges that Timothy might need to correct older believers, but he instructs him to do so respectfully, speaking to them as he would "a father" (1 Tim. 5:1).[17] Similarly, we should speak to and interact with our elders today with respect, patience, and humility, regardless of differences in opinion.

Another way we show honor to our elders is by acknowledging the physical frailty that often comes with age and responding with greater compassion. As Sklar writes, "To show such love and care for the elderly is to reflect the compassion and care of the LORD, who delights to show his love to the disadvantaged."[18]

The biblical call to honor our elders is a responsibility that believers must not take lightly. When we honor them, we are also honoring God (Lev. 19:32). If we want a strong, healthy community that benefits from the wisdom gained through years of experience, we do well to show honor and respect to our elders.

---

15 TWOT, 207.
16 Sklar, *Leviticus*, 543.
17 Sklar, *Leviticus*, 543n159.
18 Sklar, *Leviticus*, 543.

Chapter 10

After You have Suffered a Little While
(1 Peter 5:6–14)

6 Humble yourselves, therefore, under the mighty hand of God so that at the proper time he may exalt you, **7** casting all your anxieties on him, because he cares for you. **8** Be sober-minded; be watchful. Your adversary the devil prowls around like a roaring lion, seeking someone to devour. **9** Resist him, firm in your faith, knowing that the same kinds of suffering are being experienced by your brotherhood throughout the world. **10** And after you have suffered a little while, the God of all grace, who has called you to his eternal glory in Christ, will himself restore, confirm, strengthen, and establish you. **11** To him be the dominion forever and ever. Amen.

12 By Silvanus, a faithful brother as I regard him, I have written briefly to you, exhorting and declaring that this is the true grace of God. Stand firm in it. **13** She who is at Babylon, who is likewise chosen, sends you greetings, and so does Mark, my son. **14** Greet one another with the kiss of love. Peace to all of you who are in Christ.

In the closing section of his epistle, Peter continues his teaching on humility, urging his readers, "Humble yourselves, therefore, under the mighty hand of God, so that at the proper time he may exalt you" (1 Pet. 5:6). In other words, those who remain humble during their time as resident aliens in the present world will be exalted in the world to come (1 Pet. 1:5–7, 13; 14:13; 5:4). The phrase "mighty hand of God" recalls the Exodus story, where

After You have Suffered a Little While (1 Peter 5:6–14)

God delivered Israel from slavery in Egypt "by a mighty hand" (Exod. 3:19; 6:1; 13:3, 9, 14, 16).[1] In the same way, Peter reassures his readers that this same mighty hand will also deliver them. Scripture frequently highlights the theme of the humble being lifted up (Matt. 18:4; 23:12; James 4:10), and Yeshua stands as the ultimate example of this pattern (1 Pet. 2:21–25; 3:18–22). Just as he humbled himself—even to death—and was then exalted through his resurrection and ascension (cf. Phil. 2:8–9), those who walk in humility will also be exalted in due time. Meanwhile, Peter encourages believers to cast "all your anxieties on him, because he cares for you" (1 Pet. 5:7). As we devote ourselves to serving God and others with humility, we can find comfort in knowing that he lovingly carries our burdens and supplies the strength we need to persevere.

Peter continues in verses 8–10 by framing suffering within the larger context of the ultimate battle between good and evil.[2] He instructs his readers, "Be sober-minded; be watchful" (1 Pet. 5:8), echoing his earlier call to prepare their minds for action (1 Pet. 1:13). As noted earlier (see Chapter 3), being sober-minded means exercising mental discipline—that is, resisting distractions and temptations that might pull us back into a sinful way of life (1 Peter 4:3–4). Believers are to arm themselves with the Messiah's "way of thinking" (1 Pet. 4:1), which includes resisting sin and being willing to suffer for righteousness' sake if that be God's will. Peter also calls believers to "be watchful," using the same Greek word Yeshua used in his Olivet Discourse when he instructed his followers to stay alert for his return (Matt. 24:42–43; 25:13). Staying watchful in this context means actively doing the work the Master has entrusted to his servants, such as caring for the vulnerable, feeding the hungry, clothing the naked, and visiting the sick (Matt. 25:31–46).[3]

---

1 Duane F. Watson, "First Peter," in *First and Second Peter*, by Duane F. Watson and Terrance Callan, PCNT (Grand Rapids: Baker Academic, 2012), 119.
2 Watson, "First Peter," 120.
3 The identity of "the least of these my brothers" in Matthew 25:40, 45 can refer to all who are vulnerable, but there may also be a more specific reference to the Jewish people,

After You have Suffered a Little While (1 Peter 5:6–14)

Peter gives these instructions to be sober-minded and watchful because "your adversary the devil prowls around like a roaring lion, seeking someone to devour" (1 Pet. 5:8). Peter wants his readers to understand that they are engaged in a spiritual battle. Behind the human authorities and governments that persecute believers lies a darker, unseen force: the devil.[4] As our ἀντίδικος ("adversary"), a term meaning "enemy" or "accuser,"[5] the devil's goal is to destroy the "flock of God" (1 Pet. 5:2), seeking to devour believers just as a lion tears apart its prey. According to Duane F. Watson, "Being devoured by the devil is to renounce Christ and return to pagan ways and gods in order to stop the suffering inflicted by neighbors. When sheep are attacked by lions, some separate from the flock, and such are attacked and eaten."[6] Therefore, Peter calls his readers to cling to the Chief Shepherd so they do not separate from God's flock and leave themselves exposed (1 Pet. 5:1–5).

Given the spiritual danger posed by the adversary, believers are called to "resist him, firm in your faith" (1 Pet. 5:9). This means remaining committed to walking in Yeshua's ways, without slipping back into former sinful habits.[7] Peter offers reassurance to his readers by reminding them they are not alone: "knowing that the same kinds of suffering are being experienced by your brotherhood throughout the world" (1 Pet.

Yeshua's own "brothers" according to the flesh (cf. Rom. 9:3–5). On this view, Yeshua judges the "nations" (Matt. 25:32) based on how they treated the Jewish people. See D. Thomas Lancaster, *Chronicles of the Messiah* (Marshfield, MO: First Fruits of Zion, 2014), 4:1104–1105.

4   See Craig S. Keener: "The real enemy is not human authorities, although they may become instruments of demonic intention; the real enemy is spiritual" (*1 Peter: A Commentary* [Grand Rapids: Baker Academic, 2021], 381).

5   BDAG, 77.

6   Watson, "First Peter," 121.

7   See Watson, "First Peter," 121: "The devil's volley of slander and persecution can lead the recipients to deny Jesus Christ and revert to pagan ways. Remaining steadfast in the faith is the way to oppose the devil. It is to trust in God, who guards Christians through faith (1:5, 21) and protects the praise, glory, honor, salvation, and hope that is the outcome of their faith (1:7, 9, 21)."

After You have Suffered a Little While (1 Peter 5:6–14)

5:9). Believers can find encouragement in knowing that their brothers and sisters throughout the world are standing firm in their faith through the same trials. As Craig S. Keener writes, "Knowing that they are not alone in suffering is meant to console rather than discourage them; it is a corporate battle, not a merely individual one."[8]

Peter offers additional encouragement to persevere in the midst of suffering: "And after you have suffered a little while, the God of all grace, who has called you to his eternal glory in Christ, will himself restore, confirm, strengthen, and establish you" (1 Pet. 5:10). According to Peter, the suffering his readers are facing is only temporary, lasting for "a little while." This is reminiscent of Paul's words in 2 Corinthians 4:17–18, where he describes present suffering as a "light momentary affliction" in light of the eternal glory that awaits believers in the world to come. Just as Yeshua endured suffering and was later glorified, those who share in his suffering for the sake of righteousness will similarly share in his glory (1 Pet. 4:13).

After reassuring his readers of God's promise to restore, confirm, strengthen, and establish them, Peter concludes with a doxology: "To him be the dominion forever and ever. Amen" (1 Pet. 5:11). The term κράτος ("dominion") refers to God's sovereignty.[9] Believers can find solace in the fact that God's authority is supreme, and for that reason, they can rest confidently in the reliability of his promise to save them (1 Pet. 1:3–5, 9–12).

Peter concludes his epistle with the following remarks: "By Silvanus, a faithful brother as I regard him, I have written briefly to you" (1 Pet. 5:12). Silvanus was the one who carried Peter's epistle to the various communities (1 Pet. 1:1), and he may have also assisted Peter in writing it (see "Recipients" in the Introduction). Peter explains that his purpose in writing this epistle is to exhort and declare "that this is the true grace of

---

8   Keener, *1 Peter*, 389. Keener adds, "Recognizing others' sufferings was a common counsel for putting one's own sufferings in perspective."
9   BDAG, 500.

God." As Keener writes, "Peter contends that the life in Christ, despite its sufferings, is the locus of God's true grace and promise for the future."[10] For Peter, God's "grace" points to believers' ultimate salvation still to come (1 Pet. 1:10, 13; 3:7) and is what sustains them in the midst of their current suffering (1 Pet. 2:19–20). Peter urges his readers, "Stand firm in it." In other words, he wants them to remain firmly committed to the truth and refuse to turn away from the Messiah, despite suffering.

Peter writes, "She who is at Babylon, who is likewise chosen, sends you greetings, and so does Mark, my son" (1 Pet. 5:13). Just as Peter's readers are described as "elect" or chosen (1 Pet. 1:1), he also refers to another chosen community of believers located in "Babylon." In Peter's time, "Babylon" was commonly used as a cryptic reference to Rome—that is, a symbolic way to speak of the empire without naming it directly.[11] Peter also mentions "Mark," likely referring to John Mark (Acts 12:12, 25; 15:37, 39).[12]

Peter closes his epistle with the instruction to "greet one another with the kiss of love" (1 Pet. 5:14). In the ancient world, a kiss was a common expression of affection shared between family members, friends, teachers and pupils, etc.[13] By encouraging this practice, Peter is reminding his readers that they are now part of the same spiritual family, having been born again through the Messiah's resurrection (1 Pet. 1:3, 23). The letter ends much like it began: with a blessing of peace. Peter writes, "Peace to all of you who are in Christ," echoing his opening words: "May grace and peace be multiplied to you" (1 Pet. 1:2). This theme of peace in

---

10 Keener, *1 Peter*, 402.
11 See Watson, "First Peter," 126: "'Babylon' cannot be the actual Mesopotamian city, which at that time was in ruins, or the military outpost in the Nile Delta by that name, for tradition does not associate Peter with these regions. Rather, it is a reference to Rome. This association was particularly pertinent because Rome shared Babylon's idolatry and immorality."
12 Thomas R. Schreiner, *1, 2 Peter, Jude*, NAC (Nashville: B&H Publishing, 2003), 251.
13 Keener, *1 Peter*, 407–412. See also Romans 16:16, 1 Corinthians 16:20, 2 Corinthians 13:12, and 1 Thessalonians 5:26.

Messiah serves as a bookend to the epistle, affirming that even in times of hardship and persecution, believers can rest in the peace that comes from being united with him.

Lessons for Today: Stand Firm

Peter wrote this epistle to encourage his readers to "stand firm" (1 Pet. 5:12). When we are rejected, hated, and persecuted for our beliefs and values, there is strong temptation to compromise our convictions. Peter counters that impulse by reminding us of who we are: a chosen people (1 Pet. 1:1), who have been "born again to a living hope through the resurrection of Jesus Christ from the dead" (1 Pet. 1:3). This new birth secures "an inheritance that is imperishable, undefiled, and unfading" (1 Pet. 1:4). Standing firm, therefore, starts with remembering that we belong to God and that our future salvation is guaranteed if we remain faithful. Even though we face various trials as believers, we can rejoice because we have the assurance of future glory (1 Pet. 1:6–9; 5:6).

Peter also reminds us that the persecution we face as followers of Yeshua is ultimately a spiritual battle and that our "adversary the devil prowls around like a roaring lion, seeking someone to devour" (1 Pet. 5:8). Our enemy wants to destroy us and draw us away from God's flock. However, our God is more powerful than the devil, and we can cast all our anxieties on him. We are called to resist the enemy by remaining firm in our faith (1 Pet. 5:9) and humbling ourselves under God's mighty hand, knowing that he will save us at the proper time (1 Pet. 5:6).

As we conclude our study of this epistle, may we be encouraged to live out Peter's instructions. Just like his original audience, we are called to serve God faithfully in a world that rejects his ways. What does that look like? It means conducting ourselves honorably, bringing glory to the God we serve despite rejection and persecution. It means embracing suffering for righteousness' sake, following in the footsteps of our

Messiah. It means loving and serving the body of Messiah in humility and hospitality. And above all, it means setting our hope "fully on the grace that will be brought to you at the revelation of Jesus Christ" (1 Pet. 1:13). We have been born again to a living hope. May that hope shape every part of our lives as we eagerly await the salvation that is to come.

About the Author

David Wilber is an author, Bible teacher, and CEO of Pronomian Publishing LLC. He has written several books and numerous theological articles, with his work appearing in outlets such as the Christian Post and the Journal of Biblical Theology. David has spoken at churches and conferences across the nation and has served as a researcher and Bible teacher for a number of Messianic and Christian ministries.

David earned his BA in Biblical Studies from Charlotte Christian College and Theological Seminary, where he had the honor of being chosen as Valedictorian of his graduating class. He is currently working toward his MA in Religion at Southern Evangelical Seminary. In 2023, David was awarded the Dr. Eugene Kincaid Award for excellence in theology, and in 2022 he received the Zondervan Award for outstanding achievement in the study of Biblical Greek.

David currently lives in Lake Wylie, SC, with his wife and children. His work can be found at DavidWilber.com.

About the Editor

Dr. Igal German, a professor of the Hebrew Bible, offers a distinctive viewpoint as a Messianic apologist. He teaches at Moody Theological Seminary and Denver Seminary, and he leads both Yesod Bible Center (yesodbiblecenter.com) and Faith Defenders International (bibleapologist.org). His fervor for biblical scholarship and apologetics is a driving force in his work. This passion is evident in his unwavering commitment to imparting a full spectrum of knowledge to his students, fostering an environment in which they feel valued and respected, and inspiring them to delve deeper into the Scriptures. Dr. German specializes in a range of disciplines, including the Hebrew Bible in its ancient Near Eastern context and Second Temple Judaism; the biblical theology of the supernatural; the New Testament in its Jewish context; Biblical and Modern Hebrew; the history of biblical interpretation; and counter-cult apologetics.

Bibliography

Achtemeier, Paul J. *1 Peter*. Hermeneia. Minneapolis: Fortress Press, 1996.

Bai, Ying, and James Kai-sing Kung. "Diffusing Knowledge While Spreading God's Message: Protestantism and Economic Prosperity in China, 1840–1920." *Journal of the European Economic Association* 13, no. 4 (2015): 669–698.

Bailey, R. M. *Whom God Has Made Clean: A Pronomian Pocket Guide to Acts 10:9–15*. Clover, SC: Pronomian Publishing, 2025.

Bauer, Walter. *A Greek-English Lexicon of the New Testament and Other Early Christian Literature*, rev. and ed. Frederick W. Danker, 4th ed. Chicago: University of Chicago Press, 2021.

Berding, Kenneth. *Polycarp and Paul: An Analysis of Their Literary and Theological Relationship in Light of Polycarp's Use of Biblical and Extrabiblical Literature*. Vigiliae Christianae Supplements 62. Boston: Brill, 2002.

Bernstein, Brittany. "Pro-Life Activist Arrested by FBI Acquitted on Federal Charges." *Yahoo News*, January 30, 2023. https://www.yahoo.com/news/pro-life-activist-arrested-fbi-201612330.html.

Bowman, Robert M. and J. Ed Komoszewski. *The Incarnate Christ and His Critics: A Biblical Defense*. Grand Rapids: Kregel Academic, 2024.

Brazil, Scott. *Jesus and YHWH-Texts in the Synoptic Gospels*. New York: T&T Clark, 2024.

Bryant, Joseph M. "The Sect-Church Dynamic and Christian Expansion in the Roman Empire: Persecution, Penitential Discipline, and Schism in Sociological Perspective." *British Journal of Sociology* 44, no. 2 (1993): 303–339.

Bukuras, Joe. "Locked Up: Meet the Elderly and Infirm Women Now in Prison for Pro-Life Activism." *Catholic News Agency*, June 6, 2024.

Bibliography

https://www.catholicnewsagency.com/news/257916/locked-up-meet-the-elderly-and-infirm-women-now-in-prison-for-pro-life-activism.

Calvi, Rossella, and Federico Mantovanelli. "Long-Term Effects of Access to Health Care: Medical Missions in Colonial India." *Journal of Development Economics* 135 (2018): 285–303.

Capes, David B. *Old Testament Yahweh Texts in Paul's Christology*. Library of Early Christology. Waco, TX: Baylor University Press, 2017.

———. *The Divine Christ: Paul, the Lord Jesus, and the Scriptures of Israel*. Acadia Studies in Bible and Theology. Grand Rapids: Baker Academic, 2018.

Carson, D. A., and Douglas J. Moo. *An Introduction to the New Testament*. Grand Rapids: Zondervan, 2005.

Chen, Yuyu, Hui Wang, and Se Yan. "The Long-Term Effects of Protestant Activities in China." *SSRN* (2014): 1–57.

Cranfield, C. E. B. *I & II Peter and Jude: Introduction and Commentary*. TBC. London: SCM Press, 1960.

Dalton, William J. *Christ's Proclamation to the Spirits: A Study of 1 Peter 3:18–4:6*. Rome: Pontifical Biblical Institute, 1965.

Evans, Craig A. *Matthew*. NCBC. New York: Cambridge University Press, 2012.

Frostad, Benjamin. "He Made No Distinction: Gentiles and the Role of Torah in Acts 15." MA thesis, Briercrest Seminary, 2021.

Fruchtenbaum, Arnold G. *The Messianic Jewish Epistles: Hebrews, James, First Peter, Second Peter, Jude*. Ariel Biblical Commentary Series. San Antonio, TX: Ariel Ministries, 2005.

Gallego, Francisco A., and Robert Woodberry. "Christian Missionaries and Education in Former African Colonies: How Competition Mattered." *Journal of African Economies* 19, no. 3 (2010): 294–329.

González, Justo L. *Essential Theological Terms*. Louisville, KY: John Knox Press, 2005.

Goppelt, Leonhard. *A Commentary on 1 Peter*. Grand Rapids: Eerdmans, 1993.

Grudem, Wayne. *1 Peter*. TNTC. Grand Rapids: Eerdmans, 1988.

Gundry, Robert H. *A Survey of the New Testament*. 5th ed. Grand Rapids: Zondervan, 2012.

Harrington, Daniel J. "Matthew and Paul." Pages 11–26 in *Matthew and His Christian Contemporaries*, edited by David C. Sim and Boris Repschinski. New York: T&T Clark, 2008.

Harris, R. Laird., Gleason L. Archer, Jr., Bruce K. Waltke. *Theological Wordbook of the Old Testament*. Chicago: Moody Press, 1980.

Heiser, Michael S. *The Unseen Realm: Recovering the Supernatural Worldview of the Bible*. Bellingham, WA: Lexham Press, 2015.

Hillyer, Norman. *1 and 2 Peter, Jude*. NIBCNT. Peabody, MA: Hendrickson, 1992.

Himes, Paul A. *A Foreknown Destiny for the Socially Destitute: An Examination of 1 Peter's Concept of Foreknowledge in the Establishment of Social-Spiritual Identity*. PhD diss., Southeastern Baptist Theological Seminary, 2013.

House, Colin. "Defilement by Association: Some Insights from the Usage of κοινός/κοινόω in Acts 10 and 11." *Andrews University Seminary Studies* 21 (1983): 143–153.

Instone-Brewer, David. "The Eighteen Benedictions and the Minim before 70 CE." *Journal of Theological Studies* 54, no. 1 (April 2003): 25–44.

Jobes, Karen H. *1 Peter*. BECNT. Grand Rapids: Baker Academic, 2005.

Keener, Craig S. *1 Peter: A Commentary*. Grand Rapids: Baker Academic, 2021.

———. *Acts: An Exegetical Commentary*, Volume 2: 3:1–14:28. Grand Rapids: Baker Academic, 2013.

———. "Family and Household." Pages 353–368 in *Dictionary of New Testament Background*, edited by Craig A. Evans and Stanley E. Porter. Downers Grove, IL: IVP Academic, 2000.

Bibliography

Konradt, Matthias. *The Gospel according to Matthew: A Commentary*. Translated by M. Eugene Boring. Waco, TX: Baylor University Press, 2020.

Lancaster, D. Thomas. *Chronicles of the Messiah*. Vol. 4. Marshfield, MO: First Fruits of Zion, 2014.

Lankina, Tomila V., and Lullit Getachew. "Competitive Religious Entrepreneurs: Christian Missionaries and Female Education in Colonial and Post-Colonial India." *British Journal of Political Science* 43, no. 1 (2013): 103–131.

Liebengood, Kelly D. *Reading 1 Peter After Supersessionism: Jewish Apostolic Affirmation of Gentile Israelhood*. Eugene, OR: Cascade, 2025.

Luter, A. Boyd. *The Epistle of James Within Judaism: The Earliest First-Century Window into Messianic Jewish Belief and Practice*. Eugene, OR: Wipf & Stock, 2024.

Mantovanelli, Federico. *The Protestant Legacy: Missions and Literacy in India*. Paper presented at the Economic Theory Seminar, Department of Economics, University of California, Riverside, February 4, 2014.

Marjot, Oliver. *Israel, Torah and Christ in Matthew and Romans: A Conversation "within Judaism"*. PhD diss., St Catharine's College, 2022.

McKee, J. K. *Israel in Future Prophecy: Is There a Larger Restoration of the Kingdom of Israel?* McKinney, TX: Messianic Apologetics, 2013.

McKnight, Scot. *1 Peter*. NIVAC. Grand Rapids: Zondervan, 1996.

Michaels, J. Ramsay. *1 Peter*. WBC. Waco: Word, 1988.

Oliver, Isaac W. *Torah Praxis after 70 CE: Reading Matthew and Luke-Acts as Jewish Texts*. Wissenschaftliche Untersuchungen zum Neuen Testament II/355. Tübingen: Mohr Siebeck, 2013.

Panning, Armin J. "What Has Been Determined (ἐτέθησαν) in 1 Peter 2:8?" *Westminster Theological Journal* 98 (2001): 48–52.

Reeves, Jim. "This World Is Not My Home." Recorded January 28, 1962. Track 1 on We Thank Thee. RCA Victor LSP-2610, 1962. Vinyl LP.

Robinson, John A. T. *Redating the New Testament*. Philadelphia: Westminster, 1976.

Runesson, Anders. *Divine Wrath and Salvation in Matthew: The Narrative World of the First Gospel.* Minneapolis: Fortress Press, 2016.

Sabuin, Richard. "Sabbath in the General Epistles." Pages 215–228 in *The Sabbath in the New Testament and in Theology: Implications for Christians in the Twenty-First Century*, edited by Ekkehardt Mueller and Eike Mueller. Silver Spring, MD: Biblical Research Institute, 2023.

Schreiner, Thomas R. *1, 2 Peter, Jude.* NAC. Nashville: B&H Publishing, 2003.

Shelley, Bruce L. *Church History in Plain Language.* 4th ed. Grand Rapids: Zondervan, 2013.

Skarsaune, Oskar. *In the Shadow of the Temple: Jewish Influences on Early Christianity.* Downers Grove, IL: IVP Academic, 2002.

Sklar, Jay. *Leviticus.* ZECOT. Grand Rapids: Zondervan, 2023.

Sloan, Paul T. *Jesus and the Law of Moses: The Gospels and the Restoration of Israel within First-Century Judaism.* Grand Rapids: Baker Academic, 2025.

Solberg, R. L. *Torahism: Are Christians Required to Keep the Law of Moses?* 2nd ed. Franklin, TN: Williamson College Press, 2022.

Soulen, R. Kendall. "Supersessionism." Pages 413–414 in *A Dictionary of Jewish-Christian Relations*, edited by Edward Kessler and Neil Wenborn. New York: Cambridge University Press, 2005.

Staples, Jason A. *Paul and the Resurrection of Israel: Jews, Former Gentiles, Israelites.* New York: Cambridge University Press, 2024.

———. "'Rise, Kill, and Eat': Animals as Nations in Early Jewish Visionary Literature and Acts 10." *Journal for the Study of the New Testament* 42, no. 1 (2019): 1–15.

———. *The Idea of Israel in Second Temple Judaism: A New Theory of People, Exile, and Israelite Identity.* New York: Cambridge University Press, 2021.

———. "What Do the Gentiles Have to Do with 'All Israel'? A Fresh Look at Romans 11:25–27." *Journal of Biblical Literature* 130, no. 2 (2011): 371–390.

Ten Boom, Corrie. *The Hiding Place*. Grand Rapids: Baker Publishing Group, 2006.

Wahlen, Clinton. "Peter's Vision and Conflicting Definitions of Purity." *New Testament Studies* 51, no. 4 (2005): 505–518.

Waters, Guy. "Does 1 Peter 3:19 Teach That Jesus Preached in Hell?" *The Gospel Coalition*, October 21, 2019. https://www.thegospelcoalition.org.

Watson, Duane F. "First Peter." In *First and Second Peter*, by Duane F. Watson and Terrance Callan. PCNT. Grand Rapids: Baker Academic, 2012.

Wilber, David. "A New Testament Case for Christian Sabbath Observance." In *An Introduction to Pronomianism: Essays on One Torah Theology in Modern Christianity*. Jefferson, NC: McFarland & Company, forthcoming.

———. *How Jesus Fulfilled the Law: A Pronomian Pocket Guide to Matthew 5:17–20*. Clover, SC: Pronomian Publishing, 2024.

———. *Remember the Sabbath: What the New Testament Says About Sabbath Observance for Christians*. Clover, SC: Pronomian Publishing, 2022.

———. "Sabbath Observance in Luke-Acts: Situating the Earliest Followers of Jesus within Judaism." *E-Journal of Religious and Theological Studies* 11, no. 3 (2025): 51–59.

www.ingramcontent.com/pod-product-compliance
Lightning Source LLC
Chambersburg PA
CBHW070122100426
42744CB00010B/1901